CLASSICS IN EDUCATION
Lawrence A. Cremin, General Editor

☆ ☆ ☆

THE REPUBLIC AND THE SCHOOL
Horace Mann on the Education of Free Men
Edited by Lawrence A. Cremin

AMERICAN IDEAS ABOUT ADULT EDUCATION
1710–1951
Edited by C. Hartley Grattan

DEWEY ON EDUCATION
Introduction and Notes by Martin S. Dworkin

THE SUPREME COURT AND EDUCATION
Edited by David Fellman

INTERNATIONAL EDUCATION
A Documentary History
Edited by David G. Scanlon

CRUSADE AGAINST IGNORANCE
Thomas Jefferson on Education
Edited by Gordon C. Lee

CHINESE EDUCATION UNDER COMMUNISM
Edited by Chang-tu Hu

CHARLES W. ELIOT AND POPULAR EDUCATION
Edited by Edward A. Krug

WILLIAM T. HARRIS ON EDUCATION
(in preparation)
Edited by Martin S. Dworkin

THE *EMILE* OF JEAN JACQUES ROUSSEAU
Selections
Translated and Edited by William Boyd

THE MINOR EDUCATIONAL WRITINGS OF
JEAN JACQUES ROUSSEAU
Selected and Translated by William Boyd

PSYCHOLOGY AND THE SCIENCE OF EDUCATION
Selected Writings of Edward L. Thorndike
Edited by Geraldine M. Joncich

THE NEW-ENGLAND PRIMER
Introduction by Paul Leicester Ford

BENJAMIN FRANKLIN ON EDUCATION
Edited by John Hardin Best

THE COLLEGES AND THE PUBLIC
1787–1862
Edited by Theodore Rawson Crane

TRADITIONS OF AFRICAN EDUCATION
Edited by David G. Scanlon

NOAH WEBSTER'S AMERICAN SPELLING BOOK
Introductory Essay by Henry Steele Commager

VITTORINO DA FELTRE
AND OTHER HUMANIST EDUCATORS
By William Harrison Woodward
Foreword by Eugene F. Rice, Jr.

DESIDERIUS ERASMUS
CONCERNING THE AIM AND METHOD
OF EDUCATION
By William Harrison Woodward
Foreword by Craig R. Thompson

JOHN LOCKE ON EDUCATION
Edited by Peter Gay

CATHOLIC EDUCATION IN AMERICA
A Documentary History
Edited by Neil G. McCluskey, S.J.

THE AGE OF THE ACADEMIES
Edited by Theodore R. Sizer

HEALTH GROWTH, AND HEREDITY
G. Stanley Hall on Natural Education
Edited by Charles E. Strickland and Charles Burgess

TEACHER EDUCATION IN AMERICA
A Documentary History
Edited by Merle L. Borrowman

Teacher Education in America

A DOCUMENTARY HISTORY

Edited, with and Introduction and Notes, by
MERLE L. BORROWMAN

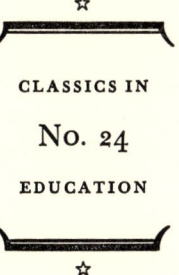

CLASSICS IN

No. 24

EDUCATION

TEACHERS COLLEGE PRESS
TEACHERS COLLEGE, COLUMBIA UNIVERSITY
NEW YORK

© 1965 by Teachers College
Columbia University

Library of Congress Catalog Card
Number 65-17004

LB
1715
.B67

Printed in the United States of America
by the William Byrd Press, Inc.
Richmond, Virginia

Preface

"The insistent present has many voices," Professor Borrowman remarks concerning the recent history of American teacher education. So also, he might have added, has the more distant past. For if there be any single theme that characterizes the documents he brings together in this volume, it is the diversity of view that has marked a century of debate over the proper preparation of teachers. From the earliest decades of the nineteenth century, when colleges, academies, grammar schools, and normal schools struggled valiantly to staff a burgeoning popular school system, Americans have disagreed among themselves about the qualities of good teachers and the best modes of nurturing those qualities. The sharp controversy that followed the appearance of Dr. Conant's report on *The Education of American Teachers* in 1963 was neither unexpected nor novel; it was merely the latest skirmish in a war that had gone on for generations.

The reasons for the conflict, of course, are not difficult to locate. If one believes, with Victor Cousin, that as the teacher goes so goes the school, then the preparation of teachers becomes a decisive element in the shaping of any school system. And inasmuch as men disagree on the ends and means of education, they will inevitably disagree on the preparation of teachers. Thus, it is no surprise that as education has moved increasingly to the forefront of public affairs, teacher education has become a matter of spirited political controversy. The conflict is both external, among segments of the public, and internal, among the educators themselves. And like all conflicts over educational policy, it goes on in the press, in legislatures, in professional organizations, in scholarly journals, and in the councils of individual colleges and universities.

There are those, I fear, who have always tended to regard such controversy with a vague sense of impropriety, holding that true professionals ought somehow to be able to resolve their differences through research instead of debate. I myself believe that continuing debate is at the heart of the matter. For as a society makes up its mind about the education of its teachers, it is really undertaking to define its own future. And while research can doubtless inform that enterprise, it can never replace the political process that is its essence.

Those who would probe further into the historical issues Professor Borrowman raises might turn with profit to Walter S. Monroe, *Teaching-Learning Theory and Teacher Education, 1890 to 1950,* Frederick Rudolph, *The American College and University,* and Professor Borrowman's own book, *The Liberal and Technical in Teacher Education,* as well as to such older but still useful works as R. Freeman Butts, *The College Charts Its Course,* Willard S. Elsbree, *The American Teacher,* and Jessie M. Pangburn, *The Evolution of the American Teachers College.*

LAWRENCE A. CREMIN

Contents

LIBERAL EDUCATION AND THE PROFESSIONAL PREPARATION OF TEACHERS
    by Merle L. Borrowman   1

1. *The First State Normal School in America: The Journals of Cyrus Peirce and Mary Swift* (1839–1851)   54

2. Richard Edwards: "Normal Schools in the United States" (1865)   74

3. College and University Responsibility for Teacher Education: Addresses to the New England Association of College and Preparatory Schools (1888–1889)   84

4. Josiah Royce: "Is There a Science of Education?" (1891)   100

5. Albion W. Small: "Demands of Sociology upon Pedagogy" (1896)   128

6. John Dewey: "The Relation of Theory to Practice in Education" (1904)   140

7. Edward L. Thorndike: "The Contribution of Psychology to Education" (1910)   172

8. William S. Learned, William C. Bagley, *et al.*: "Purpose of a Normal School" (1920)   184

9. James Earl Russell: "A Summary of Some of the Difficulties Connected with the Making of a Teachers College (1924)   208

10. George S. Counts: "Break the Teacher Training Lockstep" (1935)   218

11. Commission on Teacher Education: *The Improvement of Teacher Education* (1946)   224

*Teacher Education
in America*

A DOCUMENTARY HISTORY

Liberal Education and the Professional Preparation of Teachers*

By MERLE L. BORROWMAN

THE TRADITIONAL COLLEGE AND THE EDUCATION OF TEACHERS

One can well argue that teacher education is among the oldest functions of the liberal arts college and the university. The arts degree awarded by the medieval university was, as is generally known, a certificate of admission to the guild of professional teachers. There are no more authentic educational traditions than that teacher education is the central responsibility of institutions of higher learning and that the liberal arts and literature constitute the ideal curriculum for teacher preparation. In these traditions, to be liberally educated and to be prepared to teach are equivalent. Though the nineteenth-century development of pedagogy, or *education,* as a distinct and specialized field of study radically affected patterns of teacher education, we shall not understand certain present attitudes unless we recognize some legitimacy in the view that *even on professional grounds,* traditional liberal education included the essential intellectual components of an ideal teacher prep-

* This essay in its original form was prepared for the Institute of Higher Education, Teachers College, Columbia University, in 1959.

aration program. In the Western tradition, even as far back as Plato's *Republic,* the importance of practical experience in supplementing theoretical insights was also usually recognized.

In the classical tradition, a liberal art was an art that made men free—free from the dictates of passion and prejudice, free from the natural limitations of an untutored mind, and free from the pressure for immediate production of goods and directly marketable services. It was an art whose effective employment demanded leisure to pursue the broadest implications of an idea and to examine its relationship to other ideas. Only three kinds of people had this leisure: the young, who had not yet assumed productive roles in society; the teacher, whose social function was bound up with the arts themselves; and the adult who had become so immersed in these studies that he found, and used for their pursuit, time not required for immediately productive functions. The school was the principal home of the liberal artist, both the neophyte engaged in learning the arts and the master engaged in practicing them.

There is also, in the Western tradition, a recurring idea that the process of learning and the process of thinking at their best are identical. While John Dewey, in emphasizing the problem-solving method, redefined these processes, he was well within that tradition in arguing that one learns to think by thinking. His predecessors would have granted this, such was their case for logic; but they would have added that one also learns to think by analyzing grammatical structure and techniques of persuasion, and by studying the mathematical sciences. They would have argued further that learning occurs through imitation and, therefore, that the student who observes the master engaged in the thinking process and

Liberal Education and the Preparation of Teachers

imitates him is learning in the best possible way. In their view, one trained to think was simultaneously trained to teach.

But the liberal arts did not constitute the entire classical curriculum. Literature and the three philosophies—mental philosophy, moral philosophy, and natural philosophy—were also included. The three philosophies eventually evolved into modern scientific, social scientific, and humanistic disciplines. The basic elements of those disciplines now considered the foundations of modern pedagogy—psychology, sociology, political science, history, and philosophy—were being taught, during the pre-Civil War period, in collegiate courses in mental and moral philosophy. If in that era one wished to know the best current thought concerning human development and learning, the relationships among social institutions, and the principles for defining the good life and the good society, he could find it in texts for these subjects. The finest statements of educational theory, including methods of teaching, were confronted in the study of Aristotle's *Ethics,* Cicero's *Orator,* and Quintilian's *Institutes of Oratory,* to mention but a few widely read sources. One conversant with these works would find current questions of school-society relationships, educational objectives, learning theory, and the pedagogical use of concrete objects and experiences extremely familiar.

In the Colonial and early national periods, then, the course of the liberal arts college probably contained the best available knowledge relevant to the education of teachers. Through the prescribed curriculum, the student was broadly exposed to this knowledge and was thus prepared, as far as he could be prior to an actual apprenticeship, for teaching. The beauty of it, from the classical point of view, was that he received this preparation without being led, through an emphasis on specific vocational goals, to narrow his concerns to matters of professional technique or to see his professional interest as separate from his need for liberal culture. Nor was he isolated as a specialist from the community of educated persons.

The preceding discussion, of course, imposes a twentieth-century rationale on the activities of men long dead. So convinced were they that the classical curriculum best prepared a man for life itself, and that it was equally relevant to any vocation, that they gave limited attention to the problem of relating liberal to professional education. It is not quite true, however, as is generally assumed, that they ignored this problem completely. As Samuel Eliot Morison tells us, the *theses technologicae,* which were favorite topics for sevententh-century college disputations, added up to the argument that a "liberal education, as contrasted with mere technical training, should prepare a man to cope with any situation."[1] At the same time, the logical theses often defended the view set forth above that the purposes of logic are the purposes of education itself. It is in these theses that we find the basic rationale for the traditional liberal arts college of the Colonial and early national periods.

Though the prestige and remuneration of teachers were such that few college graduates considered teaching as a lifetime profession, the fact that many did teach, at least for brief periods, is significant. As early as 1658, tutor Jonathan Mitchell of Harvard recommended a series of scholarships which were to augment the supply

[1] Samuel Eliot Morison, *Harvard College in the Seventeenth Century* (Cambridge, Mass.: Harvard University Press, 1936), I, 161–164, 186.

Liberal Education and the Preparation of Teachers

of town schoolmasters and "Teachers of Mathematicks," among other things.[2] In the eighteenth century, several Pennsylvania colleges encouraged their students to enter the teaching profession; and in the nineteenth century, a number of states subsidized the colleges in the hope that a greater supply of teachers would be forthcoming.

The common assumption that professors in these colleges considered "knowledge of subject matter" adequate preparation for teachers gives these men too little credit for intelligence and a sense of responsibility. It also ignores the argument set forth above that the particular subject matter taught in the colleges *was relevant on professional grounds* to teaching. Our generation is increasingly redefining the teacher's function to include provision of educational leadership, participation in curriculum planning, and artistic creation of appropriate methods for handling specific situations. We might well ponder the fact that the generation of Horace Mann, one of the fathers of professional teacher education, took it for granted that these matters should be in the hands of the educated laymen of the community, in short, in the hands of men like Mann himself, who had studied mental and moral philosophy and the classics—including educational ones—in the colleges.

By 1891, the college curriculum had been revolutionized. Yet it seems reasonable to suggest that when the Harvard philosopher Josiah Royce wrote his celebrated essay denying the existence of a "science of education,"[3] he recognized the validity of the older tradition. He suggested that a prospective teacher might find, in the many courses that succeeded the classical curriculum, elements

[2] *Ibid.*, II, 372.
[3] Josiah Royce, "Is There a Science of Education?" *Educational Review*, I (January, February, 1891), 15–25, 121–132.

of instruction which would help him acquire a sympathetic understanding of children and a sensitivity to cultural forces and values, as well as a liberal store of knowledge. But, Royce argued, the teacher would have to create his own appropriate techniques for classroom practice.

The point, in discussing the old college, is not to imply that it would be adequate for our time but rather to suggest that current discussions might be less heated and more fruitful if those who reject the present version of the old liberal arts curriculum understood and granted the legitimacy that it possesses. One does not have to be malicious or stupid to find it still attractive.

But the old college is dead. Though its defenders made repeated attempts to rescue it, it was inundated by the great wave of liberal and technical scholarship of the past century. We must now examine this phenomenon. In so doing, we shall ignore the heated arguments about ancient versus modern languages and about the specific disciplinary value of particular subjects. Interesting as these arguments are, they are irrelevant to our purposes. What *is* relevant is that the corpus of liberal arts and sciences, a case for much of which could be made on professional as well as liberal grounds, expanded to the point where no one could master it in four years—or even four lifetimes. We must also note a re-examination of the assumption that when one explicitly emphasizes the utilitarian value of learning he destroys its liberal value.

THE EXPANSION OF THE LIBERAL ARTS COLLEGE AND THE RISE OF THE UNIVERSITY

In a little more than a century the house of liberal learning has been remodeled, perhaps beyond restoration, if indeed anyone wishes to restore it. Two groups of carpenters have done the job. One group believed that the rooms dedicated to pure contemplation of truth could be subdivided to permit more specialized and fundamental study of the subbranches of each art, science, and philosophy. The second believed that each room could be enlarged to make a place for those wishing to apply their knowledge directly to the mundane affairs of men. When the house became so big that a student could tarry but a moment in each room, Charles W. Eliot and others suggested that he stay as long as he wished in the rooms of his choice.

Somehow, in this remodeling process, rooms labeled "Education" appeared. Since then, the contentious family that manages the house has argued incessantly and passionately about whether *education* belongs in the house as a liberal art or science. There are those who believe that its room should be made an annex, like other professional schools and research centers; and this group includes some who love to sit in this particular room and celebrate its virtues. Even those who consider the room appropriate suggest at times that its doorkeepers detain students too long within.

The proliferation of liberal studies was under way in the eighteenth century; in fact, some tendency in this direction could be seen earlier. Geometry and astronomy had been modernized to make them more useful to surveyors and navigators, and physics had been updated and expanded during the seventeenth century. Lectures and independent reading in history and geography appear to have come early into the curriculum of the Colonial college.

By the end of the eighteenth century, proposals to expand the curriculum and make it more functional were increasingly heard. Illustrative of these is Thomas Jefferson's proposal to enrich and modernize instruction at William and Mary. Whereas the original liberal arts faculty of the college—there was also a professor of divinity, an Indian school, and a grammar school—comprised two professors who taught languages, logic, rhetoric, ethics, mathematics, physics, and metaphysics, Jefferson's new arrangement would have provided eight professors to teach moral philosophy, natural law, international law, sculpture, painting, gardening, music, architecture, rhetoric, literature, law, political economy, commerce, history, mathematics, natural philosophy (chemistry, physics, and agriculture), natural history (zoology, botany, and mineralogy), ancient languages, and modern languages. Jefferson's proposed curriculum was obviously too broad to permit any student to do justice to every study, and he therefore recommended a policy of limited student election.

Jefferson's proposal, never adopted, was significant only in that it suggested a new line of thought; he was more successful with respect to the University of Virginia, which became the passion of his later years. As the nineteenth century progressed, essentially amateur research in the natural and social sciences increased, and in dozens of colleges throughout the land the fruits of this research were introduced into college courses. The trickle of American scholars making a pilgrimage to the German universities before the Civil War grew into a tide shortly

Liberal Education and the Preparation of Teachers 9

thereafter. A substantial proportion of these scholars argued upon their return for the educational ideal to which Daniel Coit Gilman gave explicit expression and practical implementation at Johns Hopkins University in 1876. University scholars, Gilman contended, should study "all that pertains to the nature of man, the growth of society, the study of language and the establishment of the principles of intellectual and moral conduct."[4]

Among the leaders in the movement to expand the curriculum, Charles W. Eliot of Harvard is perhaps best known. His essay on the meaning of a liberal education is one of the classic statements of the new attitude toward liberal studies.[5] Eliot noted that many subjects then considered liberal, including Greek and the newer forms of mathematics, had once been outside the sacred circle and had been forced to fight their way in over the bitter opposition of faculty members with vested interests in the older disciplines. It was time, he maintained, to admit the fields of English grammar and literature, French and German, history, political economy, and the new natural sciences. He never included *education* in this list, and in at least one public gathering, he expressed serious misgivings about it.[6] His general sympathy for the newer disciplines, however, or the practical consideration of competition from other institutions, did lead him to establish a chair of pedagogy at Harvard.

When Eliot made a case for the new disciplines, he

---

[4] Daniel Coit Gilman, "The Johns Hopkins University in Its Beginning," *University Problems in the United States* (New York: The Century Co., 1898), pp. 1–41, 55–56.

[5] Charles W. Eliot, "What is a Liberal Education?" *Educational Reform: Essays and Addresses* (New York: The Century Co., 1898), pp. 89–122.

[6] New England Association of Colleges and Preparatory Schools, *Addresses and Proceedings, 1889*, pp. 32–33.

argued it in terms of the traditional values of liberal education. The new disciplines, he contended, were equivalent to the old in their ability to develop the mental powers, expand the sympathies, and cultivate good character. These ends could not be achieved, however, by a cursory study of any subject; those studies that were selected had to be explored in depth. Any attempt to cover too broad a range of subjects would inevitably lead to superficiality in habit and in knowledge. To Eliot, the elective system, with the scholar studying fewer subjects more thoroughly, appeared to be the only logical and desirable arrangement.

Technically, the argument for curriculum expansion and the elective system did not grow up in the liberal arts college itself. (Indeed, some colleges still take pride in the fact that they have resisted the urge to ape the universities.) What happened was that a new American institution, developed from a German model, was superimposed on the liberal arts school. Nevertheless, the university's view of learning as research, as well as its hospitality to new disciplines, did seep down into the college.

Meanwhile, thousands of academies, and public high schools which succeeded them, had developed throughout the land, usurping much of the ground formerly occupied by the colleges. To a certain extent, these secondary schools had been established as alternatives to the college, attracting students of the same age and, except that they substituted what was thought to be more useful learning for advanced instruction in the classical tongues and literature, offering the same curriculum. In many regions, and in several subjects, the colleges had thus been freed, or forced, to find a higher place—a place closer to that of the university, conceived as a center of advanced research and professional education. In the process they had also begun to attract a more mature student body, a fact that often went unrecognized in the relations between faculty and students.

The research ideal, as it came to dominate the college and university, was consistent with the tradition of liberal education in several important respects. In the first place, it was based on a commitment to the pursuit of knowledge for its own sake and not on an undue concern for immediate practical results. In the second place, research was a problem-raising as well as a problem-solving activity. Though some problems led the student researcher into ever more specialized inquiries, they also often led him to examine the relationships between his ideas and those of scholars in other fields. This phenomenon has been described by Alfred North Whitehead, who has argued that the stage of precise research, if properly managed, leads to the stage of generalization, in which life is seen as a larger whole.[7] Such a consequence would certainly have been welcomed by the classic thinkers on liberal education. Perhaps Whitehead's ideal university, in which scholars move from their specialized inquiries to a more profound awareness of relationships, is associated with that seen more vaguely by Eliot and Gilman.

Toward the end of the nineteenth century, some university scholars began to argue that *education*—the study of human development, the learning process, and man's educational institutions—was a legitimate enterprise within the older framework of liberal studies. Other social institutions, and the patterns of behavior associated therewith, had become central concerns of such new

[7] Alfred North Whitehead, *The Aims of Education and Other Essays* (New York: The New American Library, 1949 [c. 1929, The Macmillan Co.]), pp. 30–38.

disciplines as political science, economics, and sociology. If the study of education were scholarly, and if it yielded valuable insights for a more rational direction of human affairs, it, too, could demand a place in the circle of liberal arts and sciences. That such a development was both possible and desirable was assumed throughout Lester Frank Ward's *Dynamic Sociology*[8] and was made very explicit by Ward's disciple Albion Small.[9] On various occasions, Presidents Frederick A. P. Barnard and Nicholas Murray Butler of Columbia and President G. Stanley Hall of Clark, to mention a few distinguished leaders in higher education, gave support to the enterprise.

One of the most ardent defenders of *education* as a liberal study was Michigan's William H. Payne. If one defines his terms in a particular way, a case can be made that Payne headed the first university department of education. The enthusiasm with which he defended the classical assumptions about the distinction between utilitarian and liberal education might well have put such ardent champions of the old order as Noah Porter to shame. Is it unkind to suggest that Payne, self-taught and suspect among Michigan's community of scholars, embraced the faith with the zeal of an anxious convert, compelled to convince himself and his associates of his orthodoxy? Perhaps so, since there is no compelling evidence to support such a suspicion. There is, however, abundant evidence that Payne considered *education*, as taught in the university, a liberal art or science.[10] He seldom missed an

---

[8] Lester Frank Ward, *Dynamic Sociology* (New York: D. Appleton and Co., 1883).

[9] Albion W. Small, "Demands of Sociology upon Pedagogy," in National Educational Association, *Addresses and Proceedings, 1896*, pp. 174–184.

[10] See William H. Payne, *Contributions to the Science of Education* (New York: Harper and Brothers, 1887), *passim*.

Liberal Education and the Preparation of Teachers

opportunity to insist that the technical training appropriately offered immature students in the normal schools, who could be expected to become competent craftsmen, at best, was fundamentally different from the liberal-professional education offered potential educational leaders in the university.

Regardless of how we evaluate Payne, highly respected university scholars at the turn of the century did give attention to the problems of education. William James, James McKeen Cattell, John Dewey, Paul Monroe, Edward L. Thorndike, Albion Small, Thorstein Veblen, and G. Stanley Hall come readily to mind as illustrative. For a number of them, the study of education was obviously but one interest among many.

It must be noted that some normal-school people, among them, John Ogden[11] and Thomas J. Gray,[12] shared the view that the study of education should be scholarly and scientific, but their institutions did not generally move toward implementing this idea. A few of the early normal schools did, however, try to develop programs which presupposed a reasonable prior exposure to liberal culture, programs which were based on standard college texts in mental and moral philosophy and oriented toward the study of fundamental principles of philosophy and psychology, as then understood.[13]

The notion that *education* is a legitimate social science

---

[11] See American Normal School Association, *American Normal Schools: Their Theory, Their Workings, and Their Results, as Embodied in the Proceedings of the First Annual Convention of the American Normal School Association* (New York: A. S. Barnes and Burr, 1860) for a discussion of such trends.

[12] Thomas J. Gray, "Report of the 'Chicago Committee' on Methods of Instruction and Courses of Study in Normal Schools," in National Educational Association, *Addresses and Proceedings, 1889*, pp. 570–587.

[13] *Ibid.*

continues to excite some teacher-educators. The University of Chicago has, in the very organization of its faculty, operated on this assumption,[14] and some schools—among them, Wisconsin, Columbia, and Pomona—have devised courses in education for students who have a general interest in the school as a social institution but who do not intend to become professional teachers. Gordon C. Lee, who taught the course at Pomona, and who has written a text for it, makes the case in this manner:

> Of recent years the study of education as a social institution has increasingly been recognized as an important, indeed a vital, part of general education. Just as government, economics, and in some cases religion have been presented as basic elements in the understanding of cultures, so now education, certainly not the least of these, is emerging as one of the essential areas with which the educated man should be familiar.[15]

Some critics of teacher education, aware of the early enthusiasm for the scholarly and scientific study of education in the university, have, of course, been greatly disappointed with the results so far. When Abraham Flexner wrote his volume on American and European universities, he noted that some professions are such that a disinterested study of them is quite consistent with the liberal function of the university; of education, he was not certain. He suggested that the field had been opened with considerable promise by scholars in the best university tradition. He felt, however, that it had subsequently degenerated in the hands of mediocre people with a pas-

---

[14] See Edgar Z. Friedenberg, "Education as a Social Science," in American Association of University Professors, *Bulletin*, XXXVII (Winter, 1951), 672–692.

[15] Gordon C. Lee, *An Introduction to Education in Modern America* (Rev. ed.; New York: Henry Holt and Co., 1957), p. ix.

sion for technical know-how. The case for *education* as a liberal study could "hardly be made."[16]

In one of his early essays on the subject, Arthur Bestor, a more recent critic of professional teacher education, also observed that the study of education had been begun by competent scholars, who attempted to apply the insights of the liberal arts and sciences to professional problems.[17] His disillusionment with subsequent trends, however, appears to be complete. The study, he argued, fell into the hands of professors who "did not offer to deepen a student's understanding of the great areas of human knowledge, nor to start him off on a disciplined quest for new solutions to fundamental intellectual problems. They did not believe in preparing him for his professional activity by enlarging the store of information and insight upon which he could draw in meeting practical problems."[18]

So far, we have spoken of university reform within the context of the demand for research in all fundamental subjects, noting that for some, *education* was as much a liberal study as were the other new social sciences. Late nineteenth-century university reform, however, was not limited to the new emphasis on research. Just as significant was the more open acceptance of utilitarian values as equal in importance to the traditional liberal values and, indeed, as fully compatible with them. So far as teacher education is concerned, the belief in a highly technical program, for which immediate practical results provide the highest justification, developed largely within the normal-school tradition. Nevertheless, had the

[16] Abraham Flexner, *Universities: American, English, German* (New York: Oxford University Press, 1930), p. 29.
[17] Arthur E. Bestor, "Liberal Education and a Liberal Nation," *The American Scholar*, XXI (Spring, 1952), 139–149.
[18] *Ibid.*, p. 143.

universities themselves not come to value immediate utility, it is doubtful that their own teacher education programs could have evolved as they have.

The campaign to bring "useful knowledge" into America's institutions of higher education dates back to the Colonial era. We have already noted that geometry and astronomy, as taught in Colonial Harvard, were modified to make them more useful to surveyors and navigators. When King's College (Columbia) was being organized in 1754, its president, Samuel Johnson, proposed a curriculum including surveying, navigation, husbandry, mineralogy, geography, commerce, government, and "everything *useful* for the comfort, the convenience, and the elegance of life."[19]

While this proposal did not materialize, King's College and the College of Philadelphia were strongly influenced by the utilitarian commitments of Johnson, William Smith, and Benjamin Franklin. Their spirit flourished in the eddies of early nineteenth-century higher education and was represented in the establishment of technical institutes such as Rensselaer and scientific schools such as Yale's Sheffield School. At a few liberal arts colleges, most notably at Union College under the presidency of Eliphalet Nott, the alleged incompatibility of liberal and useful knowledge was increasingly called into question. One of Nott's students, Francis Wayland, became a lead-

[19] See John S. Brubacher and Willis Rudy, *Higher Education in Transition* (New York: Harper and Brothers, 1958), pp. 18–21, for a discussion of this and similar proposals. Indeed, this volume is useful in tracing most of the important trends in American higher education. Cf. R. Freeman Butts, *The College Charts Its Course* (New York: McGraw-Hill Book Co., 1939) for another treatment of such trends, particularly in the liberal arts colleges, and Frederick Rudolph, *The American College and University: A History* (New York: Alfred A. Knopf, 1962), perhaps the best one-volume history of the American college.

ing spokesman for the reform of the colleges in the interest of professional and practical learning.[20]

Wayland insisted that despite their protestations to the contrary, the colleges had always been professional schools, especially designed to prepare students for the ministry. But they were ill conceived, he maintained, as far as the interests of students destined for other vocations were concerned. Those destined for leadership in any occupation—including manufacturing, commerce, and teaching—required higher education tailored to their vocational needs. Wayland evidently assumed that such vocational preparation could simultaneously serve the traditional liberal functions of the colleges.

During the last half of the nineteenth century, this view became common, despite the protests of such men as Noah Porter, James McCosh, and Andrew Fleming West. The battle for useful learning was carried in the new Midwestern state universities by the advocates of instruction in agriculture and engineering, who insisted that such learning was compatible with liberal education. The sturdy yeomen of the old Northwest might tolerate "fancy learning," but not at the expense of the kind of information that would help them harvest more abundant crops. Given the egalitarian and often openly anti-intellectual bias of the Western frontier, it is remarkable that they retained enough respect for higher culture to establish universities at all. Having established them, they proposed to use them to their own ends. The nice philosophical distinctions of a Porter or McCosh were probably lost on many Western legislators and trustees.

Though not a Midwesterner, Ezra Cornell, a hard-working craftsman and part-time farmer who had fought

[20] Francis Wayland, *Thoughts on the Present Collegiate System in the United States* (Boston: Gould, Kendall, and Lincoln, 1842).

his way to the top of the telegraph empire, nicely represented the attitudes of those who controlled the new universities. His partner in the establishment of Cornell University, Andrew Dickson White, explained the values he had discovered in the European universities in terms of a long-range utility of scientific and humanistic research. Cornell, on the other hand, and others like him, believed that *immediate* utility was an appropriate educational goal. Moreover, through the Morrill Act, the federal government had given substantial encouragement to education in agriculture and the mechanical arts. People who turned to their universities for information in these fields would hardly balk at using them to augment the supply of teachers for a rapidly expanding common-school system. It is not surprising, therefore, that the new universities moved quickly into the field of teacher education or that a president of Cornell, Charles Kendall Adams, first urged the New England Association of Colleges and Preparatory Schools to see that pedagogical instruction was provided in the colleges and universities.[21]

Nor are we surprised to find that a representative of the older Eastern colleges, W. C. Poland of Brown, led the opposition to Adams' argument. Poland contended, as would be expected, that the traditional B.A. degree, which required study of the "laws of the mind," was in fact a teachers' degree. If there were certain specialized technical skills that the professional teacher had to learn, he argued, these should be taught in a separate graduate school.

Such, briefly outlined, was the tradition of the liberal arts college and the university, as it affected the profes-

[21] Charles Kendall Adams, "The Teaching of Pedagogy in Colleges and Universities," in New England Association of Colleges and Preparatory Schools, *Addresses and Proceedings, 1888*, pp. 17–29.

Liberal Education and the Preparation of Teachers

sional education of teachers. Had American teacher education developed exclusively within these institutions, the boundaries of our present arguments, in so far as they are historically defined, would thus be determined. But this was not the case. Of at least equal importance was the tradition of the American normal school, to which we must now turn.

THE TRADITION OF THE AMERICAN NORMAL SCHOOL

The American normal school, inspired by European models but developed as an intimate companion to the American common school, deserves the principal credit for establishing the ideal that teaching, on the elementary- and secondary-school levels, should command the prestige and commitment to service usually characterized as "professional." Those who advocated this ideal assumed that it could be achieved only when teacher preparation programs were placed in specialized, single-purpose institutions. If such programs were offered in a university, as came to be the case, those who retained the normal-school orientation would insist on a high degree of autonomy for the department or school of education.

More than any other institution, the American normal school glorified and supported the ideal of superb craftsmanship in classroom management. Unlike the liberal arts college and university, it was seldom at war with the lower schools for which it prepared teachers or with the lay public which it served. When in the late nineteenth and early twentieth centuries it came to entertain visions of academic aggrandizement, it still sought only to be a "people's college," tied closely to the local community and eager to serve students without any special desire for the high-brow culture of the traditional colleges. The fact that the normal school has become, for some, a symbol of illiberal study and excessive technicalism should not blind even its enemies to the power and influence it exerted. Indeed, that power and influence may well have been a function of the very tendencies many now deplore.

The pure normal school has, of course, virtually passed from the American scene. Only Wisconsin, with its system of county teachers colleges, maintains a significant number of two-year teacher preparation schools. New Jersey still has four-year colleges designed essentially as teacher-preparing institutions, but the overwhelming trend is toward converting the teachers colleges into multi-purpose state colleges. Yet important leaders in American teacher education have their roots planted firmly in the normal-school tradition, large numbers of elementary- and secondary-school teachers retain the values inculcated by the normal schools, and a number of ideas central to the normal-school tradition have been institutionalized in university programs of teacher education.

Let us examine the rationale for the nineteenth-century normal school. To do so, we must look at the situation in New England, New York, New Jersey, and Pennsylvania during the pre-Civil War era. The Midwestern and Far Western normal schools, having been established later, were never really pure forms. The very name of one of Illinois's first and greatest teacher education institutions, Illinois Normal University, nicely symbolizes the later attempt to stand between the pure normal school and the emerging state university.

As has been suggested, the normal-school campaign in the Northeast was inseparable from the campaign to

Liberal Education and the Preparation of Teachers

establish a mass system of public schools dedicated to moral and civic education. When Horace Mann became secretary of the new Massachusetts State Board of Education, his state was already blessed with a reasonably large number of secondary schools and colleges, which provided higher culture for those destined for social leadership. It was the children of the newly enfranchised mass of workingmen, the children in the rural areas, and the children of the new immigrant groups who were being sorely neglected. To be sure, Mann and others like him were so concerned with the threat of group conflict that they bitterly opposed the development of separate schools for members of particular economic classes, churches, or ethnic groups; the desire to bring the children of all such groups together in a common school was central in their thinking. But for our purposes, the significant fact is that Mann had no hope that the existing secondary schools and colleges could train the number of teachers required for the new common schools.

There were several reasons why Mann and his contemporaries considered existing academies and colleges inadequate for this assignment. The one cited most explicitly was that the teachers in such schools were too thoroughly committed to nontechnical education. Professional training—and the word "training" is used advisedly—could expect little serious support from such people, it was argued. And there was some evidence to justify this view. Franklin had complained that the Latin grammar department of his academy had overwhelmed the English school, and those who studied New York's attempt to subsidize teacher education in her academies felt that the faculties of those institutions showed little respect for the technical aspects of teacher preparation.

Moreover, graduates of the existing academies and colleges usually abandoned the profession of teaching rather quickly, if they entered it at all. Perhaps the fact that such schools attracted students who, because of social-class background or unusual intellectual interests, were promised success in more lucrative vocations was the controlling one. Possibly no amount of indoctrination concerning the great opportunities for service in the common schools could have turned such students to the teaching profession at that time.

The normal schools, on the other hand, recruited a class of students who had limited opportunities for advanced education elsewhere or for achievement in other professions than teaching. Such opportunities were especially meager in the case of girls. The rapidly expanding textile mills provided the only alternative for young women who wished to fill the years between common school and marriage with lucrative employment. If a person had a passion for serving humanity through teaching, as was sometimes the fortunate case, the normal school provided a quick entrée. Even if the passion did not exist, the singleness of purpose that characterized the normal schools gave them something of the climate of a religious retreat, well conceived to build a sense of dedication.

It appears that the early normal-school leaders had little hope, if they considered the possibility at all, that the majority of graduates would assume educational leadership, which was still a function of talented amateurs like Mann. Most of them would remain in the classroom, teaching a curriculum prescribed by the board of education, through texts selected by that board or provided on a chance basis by parents, and according to methods suggested by master teachers or educational theorists, most of whom had been educated in the colleges.

Liberal Education and the Preparation of Teachers

Given students with limited knowledge, even of the elementary subject matter they would be required to teach, and a brief period of from six weeks to two years to train them, little could be expected of the normal school. It was perhaps enough to hope that the student could be made a master of the elementary-school subjects, given a "bag of tricks"—the more sophisticated title was "the art of teaching"—by means of which his knowledge could be transmitted, and provided with an opportunity to practice his art under supervision.

There were some normal-school people who resented these limited aims. William F. Phelps, for example, principal of the Trenton (New Jersey) Normal School, frequently argued that the normal school should provide an advanced liberal education in both the general and professional areas. But he was constantly brought up short by the realization that his students were too ignorant of elementary knowledge to permit this.[22] On the other hand, the restriction of the normal-school curriculum was explicitly supported in many cases. Mann himself appears to have favored it,[23] and as late as 1866, the Massachusetts Board of Education distinctly forbade its normal schools to offer secondary-school subjects.[24] As far as states on the Eastern seaboard were concerned, the hope

---

[22] American Normal School Association, *American Normal Schools*, p. 43. Cf. Merle L. Borrowman, *The Liberal and Technical in Teacher Education* (New York: Bureau of Publications, Teachers College, Columbia University, 1956), pp. 44–45. This book provides a far more extended treatment and detailed documentation of many of the trends discussed in the present essay.

[23] Horace Mann, "Report for 1839," *Annual Reports on Education* (Boston: Rand and Avery Co., 1868), p. 60.

[24] "Resolution of July 9, 1866"; quoted by Albert G. Boyden in *History and Alumni Record of the State Normal School, Bridgewater, Massachusetts* (Boston: Noyes and Snow, 1876), pp. 18–19.

that the normal school could develop into an advanced professional school, presupposing an adequate liberal education, was clearly utopian in the pre-Civil War era.

An equally pious hope, that the students of the normal school could be given a sense of mission and dedication to service through teaching, was more nearly realized. No desire was closer to the hearts of the normal-school people, who waxed romantic about teaching as a "profession." Pressed for a definition of a profession, they would doubtless have argued that it involved, first, a deep sense of being "called" to serve—a sense so strong that one would persist in service regardless of the difficulties entailed or the temptations of other activities—and, second, an *esprit de corps* among those "called" to the vocation. The desire to produce teachers who possessed these characteristics was the central motive of the normal school and the definitive element in what was later called the "teachers college slant." In the normal schools, said Richard Edwards, an early president of Illinois Normal University, "the whole animus of both teacher and pupil is the idea of future teaching. Every plan is made to conform to it. Every measure proposed is tried by this as a test. There is no other aim or purpose to claim any share of the mental energy of either. It is the Alpha and Omega of schemes of study and modes of thought."[25]

This desire, by isolation and emphasis to make the inculcation of a sense of calling central to the entire enterprise, led Horace Mann, Henry Barnard, and others to oppose early plans for teacher education in the academies and colleges. A century later, men such as Frederick E.

[25] National Teachers' Association, *Lectures and Proceedings, 1865*, p. 278.

Bolton were still demanding absolute autonomy for university schools of education, so that the same clear focus and singleness of purpose could be maintained.[26] At the same time, William C. Ruediger, who was debating with Bolton in the pages of *School and Society*, granted that the "pride of craft, the indispensable spirit of the teaching profession, has been the unique contribution of normal schools and teachers colleges."[27]

At their first annual convention, the normal-school principals passed a resolution claiming that teaching is a profession based on a science of education.[28] No doubt they believed this was so. Having said it, they labored to make it true, appropriating whatever scientific or pseudo-scientific knowledge the social scientists of the late nineteenth and early twentieth centuries offered. By 1900, their definition of a profession had come to include the idea that a specialized body of abstract knowledge was required of its members. If by isolating themselves somewhat from the larger community of scholars they gave this knowledge some surprising twists, this was the price they paid for maintaining the singleness of purpose that gave teachers a sense of professional calling.

By 1900, the normal-school and liberal arts college traditions of teacher education were coming together in the universities. In retrospect, we can see the development of three sets of attitudes toward the relationship of the liberal to the professional components of teacher education. One of the most popular positions on teacher

[26] Frederick E. Bolton, "What to Do with University Schools of Education," *School and Society*, LXII (December 29, 1945), 432.

[27] W. C. Ruediger, "The Sins of 1839," *School and Society*, LXII (November 3, 1945), 294–295.

[28] American Normal School Association, *American Normal Schools*, pp. 106–107.

education, which had emerged in both the normal schools and the liberal arts colleges, was that of the purists, who insisted on singleness of purpose within an institution. On the liberal arts college side, this meant that no specialized professional concerns should be allowed to distort the balance of liberal studies or to mask the objectives of general culture. On the professional school side, it meant that all instruction should be rigorously tested for its contribution to competence in classroom teaching. While the professional purist hoped for the day when prospective teachers would come to him already liberally educated, he insisted that the professional school should not dilute its efforts by trying to provide both liberal culture and professional training. Advocates of this position campaigned for a "strictly professional" normal school.

The second set of attitudes was voiced by those who believed the distinction between liberal and professional studies to be a false one. Those holding this view sought, by redefining the goals of the college, to develop principles for organizing the collegiate curriculum and teaching methods so that both liberal and professional ends would be served. Within this general position, however, there were sharp differences of opinion. Some hoped to organize the course of study around the specific professional functions of teaching, while others wanted to make general social problems the core of the curriculum.

A third set of attitudes has been expressed by those who, though granting a distinction between liberal and professional education, believe that both should be begun fairly early in the student's collegiate career and should continue throughout the undergraduate and graduate programs.

THE PURIST POSITION AND PROFESSIONAL TEACHER EDUCATION

The purist position will be recognized as continuous with that of many people in the nineteenth-century liberal arts colleges and some in the normal schools. Compare, for example, the argument of S. S. Parr, president of the NEA's Normal School Department,[29] with that advanced by J. B. Sewall before the New England Association of Colleges and Preparatory Schools.[30] In 1888, Parr complained that the normal schools were hopelessly confused because of their tendency to become multi-purpose institutions. He insisted that they should demand adequate academic preparation as a condition of admission and then provide concentrated professional training. The following year, Sewall reminded the colleges that their exclusive function was to provide liberal education. The colleges had performed their sole duty, he argued, when they had "opened the way and led their pupils over a course of study intelligently and wisely planned to the end of a liberal education . . . and when they [had] provided masters in instruction." To the universities, operating at the graduate level, should go all responsibility for professional education.

In the half-century that followed these discussions, the normal school moved from the position of a secondary school to that of a collegiate institution, and the study of education found a place in virtually every American university and in most of the liberal arts colleges. By 1965, a number of states were recruiting teachers who

[29] S. S. Parr, "The Normal-School Problem," in National Educational Association, *Addresses and Proceedings, 1888*, p. 469.

[30] J. B. Sewall, "The Duty of the Colleges to Make Provision for the Training of Teachers for Secondary Schools," in New England Association of Colleges and Preparatory Schools, *Addresses and Proceedings, 1889*, pp. 22-27.

had had five years of education beyond the high school. For the first time, perhaps, it was realistic to think that prospective teachers could obtain a relatively complete liberal education and still have time for professional education and an apprenticeship in teaching. Whereas the hopes of William F. Phelps, S. S. Parr, and J. B. Sewall had been utopian in the nineteenth century, these same hopes were quite within reason in the middle of the twentieth. Moreover, school terms had been lengthened, teachers' salaries had become more adequate, the status of teaching had been raised, and labor-saving devices had made it possible for married women to think of teaching as a lifetime career. As a result, new classes of students could be recruited for the profession. It should have come as no surprise, therefore, that in 1952 the Ford Foundation's Fund for the Advancement of Education announced its willingness to support experimental programs that would implement the purist scheme.[31]

The basic assumption of the Fund-supported Arkansas experiment was a "sharp dichotomy of general and professional preparation."[32] The same principle was at the

[31] See C. M. Clarke, "The Ford Foundation-Arkansas Experiment," *The Journal of Teacher Education*, III (December, 1952), 260–264. Cf. Willard B. Spalding, "Results of the Arkansas Experiment in Teacher Education," in American Association of Colleges for Teacher Education, *The Future Challenges Teacher Education*, Eleventh Yearbook (Oneonta, N.Y.: The Association, 1958), pp. 123-131.

[32] Clarke, "The Ford Foundation-Arkansas Experiment." For a specific statement of the assumptions underlying the Arkansas experiment and other Fund-supported fifth-year programs, as well as a description of those initiated before 1957, see Paul Woodring, *New Directions in Teacher Education* (New York: The Fund for the Advancement of Education, 1958), p. 31 and *passim*. The 1958 report of Hoyt Trowbridge, *General Education in the Colleges of Arkansas* (Little Rock, Ark.: Arkansas Experiment in Teacher Education, 1958), does not deal with professional instruction, though it provides a detailed analysis of the general education aspects of the experiment.

base of other programs, such as the co-operative programs maintained by Harvard University and a number of New England liberal arts colleges. Few of these experiments have been in operation long enough to permit a complete evaluation of them, and they cannot be compared easily to programs proceeding from other assumptions. Published assessments of the Arkansas experiment make it clear that no real test of the purist assumptions was undertaken.[33] Nevertheless, this project and others like it certainly seem to justify continued experimentation. If it cannot yet be established that both liberal and professional education are improved when they are sharply separated from each other in time, there is a similar lack of conclusive evidence to the contrary. At present, it appears likely that people will judge the issue on either emotional or logical grounds. In either case, they will reason from assumptions sanctioned by tradition or arrived at through inference from some philosophical or psychological premise that seems valid and significant to them.

THE ATTEMPT TO INTEGRATE LIBERAL AND PROFESSIONAL TEACHER EDUCATION

The term "integrate" merits examination. It is a word so charged with emotion and so encrusted with special meanings for particular groups that it is highly ambiguous, to say the least. Even in what follows, it will be seen to have diverse meanings. In educational circles, it may simply represent a series of attempts to hide conflicts over principle so thoroughly that people who must

[33] Spalding, "Results of the Arkansas Experiment in Teacher Education."

compete if the conflicts are made evident can deceive themselves sufficiently to permit cooperative action. These attempts have usually involved describing a principle or situation in such a manner that conflicting values either appear irrelevant or can be organized according to the rules implicit in the description. In many cases, the apparent integration eliminates controversy as long as the discussion remains on the general policy level but fails to prevent its breaking out on the operational front. In other cases, it seems to permit agreement on the operational level, as long as discussion of underlying assumptions is avoided.

One of the earliest schemes for integrating liberal and professional teacher education was implicit in Francis Wayland's proposed reform of the college system.[34] Wayland evidently believed that if the teacher's responsibility were defined to include public leadership as well as proficiency in the classroom, and if college officials helped the teacher acquire competence for this larger calling, then the legitimate ends of both liberal and professional education would be served. Much the same argument was advanced by Alpheus Crosby at the first meeting of the American Normal School Association.[35]

Cyrus Peirce, principal of the first public normal school, and Calvin Stowe, the educational reformer from whom Peirce received inspiration, also had a theory of integration. Their theory was superficially like that of Wayland, but fundamentally very different. They argued, as Wayland did, that all plans for teacher education

[34] Wayland, *Thoughts on the Present Collegiate System in the United States.*

[35] Alpheus Crosby, "The Proper Sphere and Work of the American Normal School," in American Normal School Association, *American Normal Schools,* pp. 25–26.

Liberal Education and the Preparation of Teachers

should start with a definition of professional competence. They differed from Wayland in that they considered craftsmanship in the elementary-school classroom, not public leadership, the standard of such competence. In a letter to Henry Barnard, Peirce wrote: "The art of teaching must be made the great, the paramount, the only concern."[36]

The Peirce position received strong support, at least until 1924, when Edgar D. Randolph related its history in *The Professional Treatment of Subject Matter*.[37] It had been partially endorsed by a committee appointed by the State of Missouri and supported by the Carnegie Foundation to survey, and make recommendations for, the reform of teacher education in Missouri.[38] The study was the first of a series of investigations which, throughout the present century, have dramatized the conflicts and weaknesses in American teacher education.

The Wayland and Peirce schemes were nineteenth-century phenomena. In the twentieth century, however, the figure of John Dewey has lurked in the background of many proposals to reform teacher education. Dewey's statements have often been used as a point of departure by people sharing a general assumption but differing significantly over the implications of it. His discussion of the relationship of liberal to professional education is a case in point.

[36] Cyrus Peirce to Henry Barnard, 1851; reprinted in Arthur O. Norton, ed., *The First State Normal School in America: The Journals of Cyrus Peirce and Mary Swift* (Cambridge, Mass.: Harvard University Press, 1926), p. 284.

[37] Edgar D. Randolph, *The Professional Treatment of Subject Matter* (Baltimore: Warwick and York, 1924).

[38] William S. Learned, William C. Bagley, et al., *The Professional Preparation of Teachers for American Public Schools: A Study Based upon an Examination of Tax-Supported Normal Schools in the State of Missouri*, Carnegie Foundation for the Advancement of Teaching, Bulletin No. 14 (New York: The Foundation, 1920).

With respect to general principles, Dewey's position is clear, and not unlike that of Wayland. The best statement of it is perhaps that prepared for the 1917 meeting of the Association of American Universities;[39] the argument was meant to apply to all kinds of professional education, including that of teachers. Here, Dewey contended that if "vocational" were identified with the "bread and butter conception," involving merely "an immediate pecuniary aim," one might well oppose the growing vocational emphasis in the colleges. If, on the other hand, "vocation" were conceived as "the calling of a man in fulfilling his moral and intellectual destiny," then the trend toward vocationalism could be glorified "as a movement to bring back the ideal of liberal and cultural education from formal and arid bypaths to a concrete human significance."[40]

Opposing a "mechanical" marking of boundaries between the liberal and the professional, Dewey looked "to such a utilization of the vocational trend as will serve to make the professional school itself less narrowly professional—less technically professional. Such a transformation is not mere pious desire. The demand for it is found already in the changed relations which the professions bear to the conditions of modern society."[41]

"Is it possible," Dewey asked, "that training in law, medicine, or engineering when informed by an adequate recognition of its human bearing and public purpose should not be genuinely liberal? Is it anything inherent in these careers that confers upon preparation for them

---

[39] John Dewey, "The Modern Trend toward Vocational Education in Its Effect upon the Professional and Non-Professional Studies of the University," in Association of American Universities, *Journal of Proceedings and Addresses, 1917*, pp. 27–31.
[40] *Ibid.*, p. 27.
[41] *Ibid.*, p. 29.

that sense of narrowness and selfishness carried by the ordinary use of the words 'professional' and 'technical'? Or is this signification due to the frequent limitation imposed upon them because of exclusion or neglect of the public interest they contain? Assuredly there is lack of imagination implied in the current identification of the humanities with literary masterpieces; for the humanism of today can be adequately expressed only in a vision of the social possibilities of the intelligence and learning embodied in the great modern enterprises of business, law, medicine, education, farming, engineering, etc."[42]

Dewey obviously assumed that if the professions were properly conceived, with their broadest social and intellectual implications made the object of deliberate inquiry, the desirable elements of both professional and liberal training would fall into place. Hence, no "mechanical" marking of boundaries would be required. His argument, therefore, is based on the notion of "integration" suggested above. Aside from this aspect of his view, which will be discussed shortly, the emphasis on the social context within which the professions operate should be noted, since we shall return to this later.

Now, as has been anticipated, followers of Dewey— some close and some more remote—drew different inferences from his position. Let us examine those of William Heard Kilpatrick, an avid disciple. In 1933, Kilpatrick discussed teacher education in *The Educational Frontier,* a volume to which Dewey himself contributed.[43] It is difficult to know the extent to which Dewey agreed with Kilpatrick's position. There is some evidence that other contributors, for example, Boyd H. Bode, John L. Childs, and R. Bruce Raup, had serious

[42] *Ibid.,* pp. 30–31.
[43] William H. Kilpatrick, ed., *The Educational Frontier* (New York: The Century Co., 1933).

reservations about it, at least in retrospect.[44] One suspects that the same was true of Dewey.

Kilpatrick proposed that the units of instruction in the teacher education curriculum be the problems of the society in which the college operates and that the method of problem-solving be utilized throughout. Particular pedagogical problems would thus emerge as elements of larger social problems, and no artificial—or mechanical, to use Dewey's term—barrier would separate the general problems from the educational ones. On the solution of both, the insights of specialized scholarship would be brought to bear as needed. As the prospective teacher, working with young students in a student-teaching situation, struggled to help them solve the social problems with which they were concerned, the need for pedagogical information would arise, and such information would be obtained. Since the solution of problems, viewed in their widest possible social and intellectual context, would constitute the entire process, that process would be liberalizing and would, at the same time, develop needed professional competencies.

The Kilpatrick view was applied in the short-lived New College experiment at Teachers College, Columbia University, between 1933 and 1939, and was implicit in an experimental program developed at Adelphi College under the guidance of Agnes Snyder and Thomas Alexander, both of whom had participated in the New College experiment. In 1937, the Association of Supervisors of Student Teaching published reports of programs at Montclair, New Jersey; Stanford University; Towson, Maryland; and Terre Haute, Indiana. Common to all these programs was an attempt to integrate general edu-

[44] This judgment is based on the writings of Bode and on personal conversations with Childs and Raup.

cation, professional education of a theoretical sort, and direct laboratory experiences.[45]

An expression of a somewhat Kilpatrick-like version of the more general Deweyan assumption can be found in a 1956 publication of the American Association of Colleges for Teacher Education.[46] The crucial chapters were written by Florence B. Stratemeyer, who had been associated with the New College project.

Miss Stratemeyer assumes, as Dewey did, that teacher education should take its departure from a definition of the teacher's role as social leader. She has also been strongly influenced by those who stress the importance of helping the individual adjust effectively to his social group. While she constantly emphasizes the importance of scholarship, she insists that it can be of value only if it is oriented toward social service. To insure that scholarship is so oriented, and that teaching proceeds in a manner consistent with the principles of learning that she accepts as valid, Miss Stratemeyer proposes that the units of instruction be problem situations resembling, as nearly as possible, the situations in which knowledge is to be applied. This means that the situations must be concrete and practical.

It is interesting to note that Miss Stratemeyer uses

[45] Supervisors of Student Teaching, *The Integration of the Laboratory Phases of Teacher Training with Professional and Subject Matter Courses*, Yearbook, 1937, edited by John G. Flowers.

[46] Donald P. Cottrell, ed., *Teacher Education for a Free People* (Oneonta, N.Y.: The American Association of Colleges for Teacher Education, 1956). Cf. National Commission on Teacher Education and Professional Standards, *New Horizons for the Teaching Profession*, edited by Margaret Lindsey (Washington, D.C.: National Education Association, 1961), pp. 27–108. The reader will note here the same concern with integration, though the argument is not so fully developed and is presented in such a way that one less committed to detailed integration might find the NCTEPS statement acceptable.

"abstract" and "functional" as opposite terms.[47] Thus, by implication, "concrete" and "functional" are nearly synonymous. Many scientists would insist that the most crucial advances in inquiry, including the development of scientific laws that have had tremendous long-range functional value, have been made by deliberately creating an abstract logical system which isolates certain factors from others that normally accompany them in concrete, practical situations. Similarly, there are those in the humanities who would argue that the most valid insights are brought into focus by abstracting certain elements from concrete events and imaginatively creating an artificial situation in the context of which these elements can be dramatically examined. It could be, then, that Miss Stratemeyer's conception, or misconception, of the terms "concrete," "abstract," and "functional" leads her to ignore some factors that others would consider essential to liberal education, despite her emphasis on the value of scholarship.

But to return to her proposals, she argues that the ideal units of instruction are situations involving the unique personality of an actor operating in a social group that shares certain fundamental conditions, needs, and problems. "The needed synthesis is achieved," she maintains, "when the situations of everyday living which students are facing are seen as aspects of continuing life situations with which all members of society must be able to deal."[48] These "immediate and continuing life situations" (e.g., understanding oneself; communicating thought and feeling; understanding and dealing with the natural and social environment as well as with current social, economic, and political problems) are, then, to

[47] Cottrell, ed., *Teacher Education for a Free People*, pp. 88, 149.
[48] *Ibid.*, p. 96.

become the organizing centers of the general education curriculum. The same general assumptions underlie her discussion of professional education.

Thus, she states as a first principle that *"experiences in the professional sequence should be selected and organized with reference to performance responsibilities*—teaching situations to be met and educational problems to be solved—rather than logical subject-matter relationships, *per se."*[49] Such problems include how to become acquainted with students and understand them, how to help them have "meaningful experiences," how to guide them in developing specific skills, how to evaluate effectively, how to work co-operatively with parents and colleagues, and how to bring about educational change. These are the "continuing life situations" relevant to the professional sequence. On their resolution, specialized scholarship would be brought to bear as needed but would not be presented in terms of its own internal logic.

From Miss Stratemeyer's point of view, it is useful to distinguish among general education, professional education, and subject-matter specialization as sources of certain competencies the citizen-teacher should have. But since these categories are not based on either the internal logic of the knowledge involved or the mode of presenting it to students, the traditional issue of *liberal versus professional* education is bypassed. Miss Stratemeyer and those who share her point of view argue that ideally all three elements of the curriculum should be carried forward simultaneously in order to provide time for the maturation of thought in each field and to prevent the student from assuming that learning of any sort is "finished" when he moves on to a new element. It is also necessary, they argue, that the professional situations be

[49] *Ibid.*, p. 150.

seen as but special aspects of the general life situations with which general education is concerned, and that the specialized knowledge be acquired with a view to its implications for these general life situations. The concrete application of knowledge is essential, even though the student approaches the specialized field in terms of its own particular logic and method of inquiry.

Miss Stratemeyer provides illustrative examples of the kinds of curricula implied by these considerations.[50] While her projected curricula go beyond anything widely found in current practice, she also cites experimental programs in both general and professional education that appear to be moving in their direction.

We have now discussed two general views on the relationship of liberal to professional teacher education. The first of these, that of the purists, allows maximum autonomy for both the professors of the liberal arts and the professors of education. The second, calling for a close integration of the general and professional programs, demands a maximum of co-operative effort and could doubtless be implemented most easily in single-purpose institutions or in colleges small enough that all members of the teaching body can be brought together expeditiously for the kind of detailed planning required if integration is to be carried out in the classroom.

An increasing number of teachers, however, are being educated in institutions where the faculty is large, and the vocational and intellectual interests of both students and faculty diverse. By 1962, such institutions were preparing approximately 90 per cent of all teachers.[51] In

[50] *Ibid.*, pp. 238–267.

[51] My estimate, based on reports gathered for James Bryant Conant's *The Education of American Teachers* (New York: McGraw-Hill Book Co., 1963), is that approximately 90 per cent of the teachers were trained in "multi-purpose" institutions preparing

these institutions, the majority of faculty members have an interest in professional teacher education that is, at best, tangential to their most active concerns. Moreover, the task of relating liberal education to the many legitimate vocational aspirations of students is a most complex one. Even those who grant that professional education is not, as such, antithetical to liberal education, and who concede the desirability of providing parallel liberal and professional courses, find it necessary to develop two sequences which have only a casual relationship to each other. Only the most general policy questions can expect the serious consideration of an entire faculty. It is hard to imagine a great state university trying to integrate its general education offerings with all the professional courses of its students according to a scheme such as that proposed by Miss Stratemeyer. What actually results, perhaps inevitably, is precisely that kind of mechanical—a better word may be "political"—allocation of credits for general education, subject-matter specialization, and professional education deplored by both Dewey and Miss Stratemeyer.

We are led, therefore, to consider the third great branch of thought about the relationship of liberal to professional teacher education: that which encourages a mutual respect for each, the establishment of parallel curricula, and such occasional references to interrelationships as individual instructors of the liberal and professional courses are disposed to make.

THE ECLECTIC OR *AD HOC* APPROACH

Since 1930, there have been two massive investigations of

---

more than one hundred teachers per year. The data are not reproduced in this form in the Conant volume.

American teacher education, dozens of national conferences on the subject, and hundreds of institutional self-studies of teacher education programs.[52] In most of these, arguments have been advanced both for separating liberal education sharply from the professional education of teachers and for closely integrating the two. But consensus in favor of either extreme position has not emerged. Several reasons for this can be suggested. One is that no institution has been able to attempt either plan under conditions that its advocates would consider sufficiently ideal for the experiment to be accepted as a definitive test of their basic assumptions. A second reason is that the educational process is simply too involved, too little susceptible to the kind of control that scientific experimentation demands, and aimed at too many different outcomes to permit its being evaluated in terms of any single theoretical principle. A third is that because of

[52] The major studies include the National Survey of the Education of Teachers, sponsored by the United States Office of Education between 1930 and 1933 and directed by Edward S. Evenden, and that of the Commission on Teacher Education, sponsored by the American Council on Education between 1938 and 1944. The summary publications of these studies are: United States Office of Education, *National Survey of the Education of Teachers*, Bulletin 1933, No. 10, Vol. VI, and Commission on Teacher Education, *The Improvement of Teacher Education: A Final Report by the Commission on Teacher Education* (Washington, D.C.: American Council on Education, 1946). For reports of three significant national conferences, see National Commission on Teacher Education and Professional Standards, *The Education of Teachers: New Perspectives*, Report of the Second Bowling Green Conference, 1958; *The Education of Teachers: Curriculum Programs*, Report of the Kansas Conference, 1959; *The Education of Teachers: Certification*, Report of the San Diego Conference, 1960. All were published by the National Education Association in Washington, D.C. (1958, 1959, 1961). James D. Koerner and James Bryant Conant have recently made rather extensive surveys with foundation support. Cf. Koerner, *The Miseducation of American Teachers* (New York: Houghton Mifflin Co., 1963) and Conant, *The Education of American Teachers*.

their different experiences, faculty members in teacher education institutions have developed strong biases at such variance with those of their colleagues that compromise provides the only means of achieving co-operation. In any case, there has been a widespread tendency to avoid pressing for agreement on a single overarching principle. Instead, there has been a willingness to seek agreement on secondary principles and on operational levels.

In describing the set of attitudes that has perhaps become most common among those concerned with teacher education, we are forced to abandon the attempt to define *the* controlling principle and be content with describing the process by which planning occurs as an eclectic one.

Nevertheless, there is a considerable body of agreement on certain operational assumptions. One of these is that an attempt should be made to secure the serious support of all faculties of the university for instruction aimed at the development of (1) liberal culture, (2) proficiency in some specialized field, and (3) professional competence. A second is that the entire faculty of the university should be involved, at least on the policy level, in determining the distribution of time among the different elements of instruction and the general structure of each. A third is that no decision with respect to any one element should be made without explicit consideration of the experience the student has had, or will have, with the others.[53] The fourth widely held operational

---

[53] Cf. United States Office of Education, *National Survey of the Education of Teachers*, VI, 75, and Commission on Teacher Education, *The Improvement of Teacher Education*, pp. 78–103. The same assumptions are supported in the more recent task force report of the National Commission on Teacher Education and Professional Standards, *New Horizons for the Teaching Profession*, pp. 27–108.

assumption is that a student needs time to mature in his consideration of pedagogical problems and should not be encouraged to think his liberal education is finished when he begins professional instruction. This is balanced by a fifth assumption, namely, that instruction should move from the clearly liberal to the clearly professional as the student approaches actual employment as a classroom teacher.

These assumptions were implicit in the report of the American Council on Education's Commission on Teacher Education.[54] Though the commission itself explicitly denied any intent to set down definitive proposals, it did, for example, stress the importance of involving the entire faculty in planning for teacher education. It insisted that a reasonable amount of time, perhaps three-eighths of the total undergraduate curriculum, should be devoted to general liberal education and that from one-eighth to one-sixth of the course should be dedicated to strictly professional instruction. It recognized that some instruction is equally relevant to liberal and professional ends, and it recommended that liberal education, subject-matter specialization, and professional training overlap each other in time.

To this point, our discussion has considered the relationship of a part of teacher education called "liberal" to a portion designated as "professional." In the earlier discussion of collegiate reform, however, it was noted that many have viewed courses in education as potentially liberal. Having discussed the relationship of the liberal *to* the professional, we must now consider the liberal *in* professional instruction. The crucial problem

[54] Commission on Teacher Education, *The Improvement of Teacher Education*.

here concerns the relationship of liberal to technical instruction within the professional curriculum.

THE LIBERAL IMPULSE IN PROFESSIONAL EDUCATION

In his 1958 address to the American Association of Colleges for Teacher Education, Paul Woodring argued that a distinction should be made in the professional curriculum between professional knowledge and professional skills.[55] In the former category he included an understanding of the child and the learning process, on the one hand, and philosophical insight into educational aims and purposes, on the other. The first, he argued, should be drawn from psychology, sociology, anthropology, and statistics; the second, primarily from philosophy, history, and sociology.

Speaking of the philosophical element, he argued that it should bridge the gap between liberal and professional education. Although the course in philosophy can be listed as a professional requirement, "its content is liberal in the best sense of the word." "In fact," he continued, "I see no good reason why it should not be required in a liberal arts college, for every educated person needs this

---

[55] Paul Woodring, "The New Look in Teacher Education," in American Association of Colleges for Teacher Education, *The Future Challenges Teacher Education*, pp. 9–25. For a more extended statement of the Woodring position, see his *New Directions in Teacher Education*. Cf. Conant, *The Education of American Teachers*. Conant does not speak of *education* as a liberal study. He does, however, insist that professors of educational history, philosophy, sociology, and psychology be "intermediary professors," that is, historians, philosophers, etc., recognized as such by their university colleagues but prepared and inclined to bring their academic disciplines to bear on educational problems.

kind of understanding of the meaning and purpose of formal education."[56]

In making the distinction between professional knowledge and professional skills, Woodring reopened one of the oldest debates in American teacher education circles. As we have seen, this very distinction separated Cyrus Peirce's "professional treatment of subject matter" position from Francis Wayland's proposal to design a professional school on the basis of the teacher's function as social leader.[57] The descriptions of Flexner and Bestor imply that American teacher education began by being largely liberal and degenerated as the technical element was allowed to overwhelm the liberal.[58] If Woodring's distinction is valid, then Miss Stratemeyer's insistence that practical life situations should constitute the basic units of the teacher education curriculum and the view of Kilpatrick and others that all elements of that curriculum should be oriented around practice-teaching situations are perhaps erroneous. Woodring, like many of the people working in the area of the "social foundations of education," evidently wants to maintain this distinction.[59] But there have always been a substantial number of people, especially among those responsible for student-teaching experiences and those whose principal interest is educational psychology, who have resented the distinction and considered it invalid.[60] Woodring described the present opposition to his position as follows:

[56] Woodring, "The New Look in Teacher Education," p. 19.
[57] *Supra,* pp. 30–31.
[58] *Supra,* pp. 14–15.
[59] See National Society of College Teachers of Education, Committee on Social Foundations, *The Emerging Task of the Foundations of Education, The Study of Man, Culture, and Education: A Statement to the Profession* (Ann Arbor, Mich.: The Society, n.d.).
[60] Cf. Borrowman, *The Liberal and Technical in Teacher Education,* p. 21.

Liberal Education and the Preparation of Teachers 45

Yet professional courses taught . . . as intellectual exercises involving reading, thinking, and discussion, but without direct contact with children, are under direct attack from two sources: first, from academic groups who doubt that education as a discipline has sufficient content to justify such courses; and, second, from those extremely "practical" people who think no course in education should be taught except in direct reference to children and with children physically present. These people have forgotten Dewey's wise statement that "theory is, in the long run, the most practical of all things." It is the most practical because it has the widest implications and the most long-range applications.[61]

THE YEARS AHEAD

Even in recounting past events one is hard pressed to separate what was from what he wishes had been. In guessing what lies ahead, a most hazardous venture at best, objectivity is even more difficult to achieve. The value of any projection into the future, however, is the guidance it gives for present action, and perhaps such action should be determined as much by what one hopes will be as by what he expects to occur.

We have described three general sets of attitudes toward the relationship of liberal to professional teacher education. That of the purists, who favor a four-year liberal education followed by a fifth year of highly professional training, has been idealized by some for a hundred years. The purist program is now for the first time a real possibility. Our economy has prospered, so we can afford to maintain potential teachers in college for five years; the status of teachers has improved enough that a class of students willing to devote five years to general and professional education can be recruited in some

[61] Woodring, "The New Look in Teacher Education," pp. 16–17.

states; and the public has become so sensitive to educational problems that it generally recognizes the need for teachers with such extensive preparation. The purist position has all sorts of attractions. It is logically neat; it is, of all schemes, the one most easily administered; and it calls for the least amount of co-operative effort among groups holding antagonistic views on educational issues. Those of us who have studied the classical tradition, with its emphasis on the need for leisure and freedom from utilitarian concerns during the period of liberal education, are inexorably drawn to this position. While views that have been held for several centuries by significant groups do occasionally pass out of favor, a careful gambling man would have to wager against their disappearance. The purist attitudes will remain.

There is sufficient plausibility to the arguments of those who hold this position and sufficient convenience in administering the plans they propose to warrant continued development of the purist program. Even if other plans are considered more ideal, the purist scheme provides a means of recruiting and preparing badly needed teachers for whom the vocational motive emerges late in their collegiate careers.

There are, however, certain important considerations that the purist position does not take into account. For one, there is justification and necessity for choice among the potentially liberal subjects a college student may take. If some of these, though taken primarily for liberal ends, are incidentally of greater professional value to the prospective teacher than others, it seems a strange sort of narrow-mindedness to ignore this consideration in planning a liberal education program. Courses in the liberal arts and sciences are not made illiberal by recognizing, though not emphasizing, their professional relevance. The Fund for the Advancement of Education implicitly acknowledged this in granting funds recently to encourage the study of educational history as one important element in American social history. To include educational history as an aspect of social history is not to make history courses less liberal; on the contrary, it simply broadens and makes more accurate the consideration of one's tradition. Yet surely a teacher is made more adequate professionally by having examined the relationships of his enterprise to the larger social milieu.

A second objection to the purist position is that it neglects the use of professional aspiration as a motive for learning. One may reasonably believe, as I do, that early vocational choice should not be forced or even unduly encouraged. But such choice does occur in many cases, and the student with a call to serve in some vocation is more highly motivated to learn if the knowledge which is presented can be seen as relevant to his calling. Devices for motivating students are not so abundant that we can wisely ignore those that are given.

A third objection is that the purist program provides too little time for the maturation of ideas about professional problems. This is a common argument, and it may be a fallacious one. Nevertheless, one gets the impression, without having tested it empirically, that considerable educational gain is derived from delayed response to particular learning experiences. One often encounters an idea the meaning of which is partly obscure or apparently superficial. Not infrequently subsequent experience, or exposure to other ideas, leads to a new and deeper understanding of that which was at first but dimly perceived. It would be well if there were time for certain ideas about teaching to mature and be tested before the prospective teacher begins his career. It may be that the single year proposed by the purists—a year during most of which the apprenticed teacher is deeply involved in all sorts of pressing practical problems—is too short a period. The issue here is not the amount of time spent under actual professional instruction but the amount of time that separates the student's earliest introduction to professional problems from his last examination of those problems before he assumes a full-time teaching job. If a single year is too short a time, however, this does not imply that the longer the period, the better. Perhaps the rather common two-year span is reasonably near the optimum in most cases.

To me, however, the most persuasive argument against the purist position is that it makes of teaching an illiberal profession. There are already enough forces tending in this direction without teacher education institutions lending a hand. Among these forces are: (1) the load of teaching and administrative detail which denies the typical elementary- or secondary-school teacher time to examine broadly the implications of his practice, to provide leadership in educational matters, or to be at all creative in his teaching; (2) the stereotype, reinforced by the normal-school tradition of teacher education, of the teacher as a skilled craftsman, at best; and (3) the low salary and prestige which confirm this stereotype. The separation of liberal from professional education too often implies that professional education is merely technical education. One hopes that we can prepare teachers who, in addition to being technically competent, are artists, creating on the basis of principles having broad general validity and evaluating educational efforts in terms of the widest social ramifications of those efforts. This means that educational theory must be perceived as continuous with other aspects of social theory, that the criteria of effective education must be seen as inseparable from the criteria of effective social and personal living, and that the techniques for inquiring into educational problems must be recognized as of the same nature as those used in other kinds of inquiry. To imply by the structure of the curriculum that professional education is essentially different from liberal education is to suggest strongly that it is technical education. In my judgment, "liberal" and "technical," not "liberal" and "professional," are the polar terms.

The purist scheme seems to damage liberal as well as professional education by suggesting that one's liberal education is finished, and should be placed on the shelf, when he turns to his vocational life. While we might well hope that mastery of the methods of inquiry that intrigue the liberal mind—the techniques of grammar, rhetoric, logic, mathematics, scientific experimentation, social science research, and normative inquiry—would be reasonably well under way before the student becomes preoccupied with his profession, surely we do not want to encourage students to abandon liberal education at the moment professional education begins.

The position of the integrators, on the other hand, is strictly utopian. The projection of grand schemes that incorporate all values into one neat rational system is useful in enabling one to examine fully the logical implications of certain basic assumptions. But as a prescription for practice, utopian thought is both unrealistic and dangerous. It is unrealistic because its implementation presupposes either consensus among all those concerned or a nearly totalitarian concentration of power in the hands of a few. A small college, especially a single-purpose one, may permit sufficient discussion and mutual persuasion for something approaching consensus to emerge. In a weak college, a very strong administrator or power elite may impose a well-integrated course of study on the institution. But a large, able faculty, each member of which has his own well-examined values and time-consuming interests, is not likely to reach the agreements necessary for achieving real integration.

Moreover, utopian integration, that is, the detailed organization of an entire liberal and professional curriculum on the basis of one or two idealized principles, is dangerous. The values to which collegiate and professional education are dedicated cannot be placed in hierarchical order. Nor does "what we know about learning," to use an expression now becoming trite, add up to a system of noncontradictory principles. When, and if, the day comes that the determination of educational means *and* ends is strictly scientific, we may be ready for utopian integration. Meanwhile, it might be safer simply to offer a wide selection of courses, some of which are dedicated to different and perhaps logically incompatible ends and premised on assumptions about learning that are implicitly denied in the way other courses are taught.

A final objection to utopian integration is that the act of integrating ought to be that of the student. A faculty that does the integrating for the students and merely transmits its conclusions to them is depriving them of the opportunity to learn by experience one of the liberal arts —that of seeking and defining interrelationships among different kinds of knowledge. Besides, since those interrelationships a faculty points out are sometimes rather obvious, an integrated program might succeed merely in boring the students.

Because the eclectic approach seems more realistic, given the size and complexity of modern universities and colleges, than the pure integrationist position, one is led to conclude that the future lies with this or the purist approach. In view of the objections set forth above with respect to the purist scheme, one might well hope that the eclectic rather than the purist position will predominate.

The eclectic approach causes a great deal of frustration for everyone involved. If the professors of the liberal arts and sciences and the professors of education are to work together in allocating credits and seeking balance among professional education, general liberal education, and specialized training in academic fields, endless committee meetings are in the offing. The resultant decisions will inevitably be less than completely satisfactory to those whose ideological positions have been carefully examined and clearly defined. All must face the fact that no one will have his way exactly. Yet I cannot escape the conclusion that liberal education will be improved if those responsible for it examine its relationship to professional education, and that the latter will be improved if it is in the hands of those who have considered the problems of liberal education and the relationship of professional to general liberal arts courses.

Even if in the long run the purist or integrationist position is adopted, the present controversy makes it clear that America's higher educators have not yet been able to make a definitive case for either one. The best way to achieve consensus is through the process of jointly hammering out tentative decisions on an institutional and *ad hoc* basis. One general axiom concerning social change might well be considered in deliberations over the reform of teacher education. It is that ideological principles are not definitive and that change occurs in piecemeal fashion. To be sure, ideological argument serves to enlist the energies of people and helps them examine the implications of their general beliefs, but on the operational level, compromise always occurs. Even in the Communist Revolution, perhaps the most thoroughly ideological revolution in history, pure Marxism has not prevailed. That it has not is due partly to its own inadequacies as a system of thought and partly to the fact that a theoretical structure necessarily ignores certain practical conditions and fails to win the complete loyalty of any group of individuals. It is hoped that teacher education theory will be tempered by a sense of reality and by a recognition that no monolithic system of thought can determine the activities of the kinds of faculty members and students involved in teacher education programs.

A NOTE ON THE READINGS

The insistent present has many voices, as it should. Those who have sought over the past few decades to conserve, criticize, or reform American teacher education can speak for themselves. I have not reproduced any of the recent extensive literature in the field, despite the obvious importance of much of it.

But the past also participates in our deliberations. It speaks subtly, and some of us are quite unaware of the cues by which it molds our thoughts and shapes our responses. But it molds and shapes nonetheless. We cannot choose whether to be conditioned by it or not; we choose only to be aware or unaware of its influence.

I have selected arbitrarily several arguments advanced during the first century of teacher education in America. I find these particular selections interesting because their authors were thoughtful people, because they spoke at a time when critical decisions concerning the education of American teachers were being made, or because they represented a major emphasis in American teacher education.

1. *The First State Normal School in America: The Journals of Cyrus Peirce and Mary Swift**
(1839–1851)

Cyrus Peirce was principal of the first public normal school in America, which was established at Lexington, Massachusetts, in 1839, and later moved to West Newton. On its success rested the hopes of all those who had long urged the creation of professional schools for teachers. Its failure might have seriously threatened the entire common-school movement in New England.

Peirce was prepared for this pioneering venture by several years of teaching in private and public schools and by attending Harvard College, from which he had received both a baccalaureate and a divinity degree. He had also served as a Unitarian minister. In training and experience, then, he was like many other professional teachers in the Boston area. But Peirce considered himself "called" to lead a noble experiment. In its singleness of purpose, its evangelical zeal, and even its commitment to dogma, his normal school resembled the divinity schools that trained the missionaries of militant, fundamentalist, Protestant sects. Whether the twenty-five adolescent girls who attended his first class felt a "calling" on entering the school cannot be said. We do know that most of them left as dedicated missionaries of public education.

* Edited, with an Introduction by Arthur O. Norton (Cambridge, Mass.: Harvard University Press, 1926).

Among those first twenty-five was Mary Swift, who, from the time she entered Lexington at the age of seventeen until her retirement many decades later, apparently never doubted that to be a teacher of children is a most serious, noble, and inspiring work. Her journal, a portion of which follows, is that of an eager, conscientious, and perceptive student. Her career is the stuff of which the best case for the American normal school has been made.

The Peirce letters were written at the request of Henry Barnard, the leader of the common-school movement in Connecticut. Perhaps Horace Mann deserves the credit usually given him for being a more effective campaigner for educational reform than Barnard. But one interested in the long-range development of professional education in America cannot fail to recognize that it was Barnard who led in gathering and disseminating reliable information on which effective educational judgments could be based.

JOURNAL OF MARY SWIFT*
(1839)

Tuesday [13th][1] This day would seem hardly to need a separate account the exercises thereof so nearly coincide with those of Monday—Mr P. instead of hearing our lesson in N. Philosophy explained it to us & deferred our recitation until tomorrow morn.—

Wednesday [14th] We recited the lesson which was explained yesterday on the subject of Vision. On opening the school Mr P. made some remarks on the manner in

* *The First State Normal School in America,* pp. 88–92.
[1] August.—M. L. B.

which the words prevent & let were used in the bible, as differing from their present use. The lesson in Physiology was a review of the 3d Chap. upon various subjects but especially recommending the use of the bath & teaching the manner in which it should be used.—After reciting a short lesson in Political Economy the school closed the lesson in N. History being deferred until the next day — — —In the P. M. spent an hour in writing home & after mailing the letter met Mr P. who gave us an invitation to attend the fair at the East Village. We accepted & had gone as far as the Monument House, when we met Mr Morse the preceptor of the High School in Nantucket.— He was intending to return to Boston in a short time & Mr P. stopped to speak with him, promising to overtake us before we got to the Village. He did so, and accompanied us up to the scene of action—Upon the hill called Mt. Independence was a building which appears to have been erected for an observatory—It was prepared for the refreshment table, and hung with evergreens. To contain the articles for sale large tents were made covered with canvass—adjoining this was a tent at right angles in which a long table was set for the entertainment in the eve.— — — —There were many people from the neighboring villages & all the tents were crowded—Groups were scattered among the trees and others were standing at the edge of the hill admiring the scenery around & below.- — — —After viewing the fancy articles we entered the observatory & went into the upper part where Mr P. named many of the hills around & showed us the state of New Hampshire, & the commencement of the White Mountains. We also saw the ocean but it was at so great a distance that it appeared like mist over the land.—When we had become wearied with standing we descended to the refreshment room, where Mr P. treated us to ice-cream & cake—Contrary to the principles of Blakewell's Philosophy, we felt much cooler after eating the cream. —We sauntered through the grove & again through the tents, when it grew dark & we returned home, very well pleased with our afternoon excursion.—Went to tea with Mrs Muzzy in company with Miss Stodder's sister who had just come out from Boston.—

Thursday [*15th*] Our lesson in Philosophy was upon the subject of vision—Physiology upon the Muscles— Political Economy upon the objects of the work, & Natural History was deferred. In the P.M. we read from Abbotts Teacher on the subject of making the lessons which we attempt to learn familiar.—The lessons in Pronunciation & Orthography were well recited & the school closed with a short recitation in Music——

Friday [*16th*] This morn, Mr Peirce wished to try the experiment of having one of the scholars hear the recitation in N. Philosophy. Accordingly he gave to me the charge of the recitation. The feeling caused by asking the first question tended rather to excite my risibles, but feeling the necessity of sobriety—I was enabled to play the teacher for a short time. I think that he can judge very little about our idea of teaching from the example which we give him in hearing a recitation for the manner in which it is carried on depends very much upon the interest felt by the teacher in the scholars & in their study.—To furnish a variety in conducting a recitation I think it will answer very well. Our lesson in Physiology was conducted on a different principle that of learning the lesson & then writing an abstract which we read instead of recitation—During the exercise Mr Thompson from Nantucket came in & passed the remainder of the forenoon with us. The exercises were Political Economy & Natural History; neither of which were well recited.—

The afternoon passed like the preceding & after tea I called to see Miss Starbuck from Nantucket who is here on a visit.—

Saturday [*17th*] This morn after the recitation in Orthography, & the solution of a few problems on the Globe, Mr P. gave his weekly lecture.—He commenced by giving a brief abstract of the preceding lecture. He then stated the subject of the present: "the motives, qualifications & responsibilities of a teacher".—the motives by which a teacher should be influenced are various, 1st I will give the negatives. We often hear it said that such a person is qualified for nothing else. We should then be led to think that she was qualified for that but poorly—Inadequacy in common trades, is felt only by the person himself, but in the teacher, its consequences are felt by the pupils, & their influence does not only extend to this moment or year, but is felt in succeeding generations. As in the constructions of a watch, of an inconvenient house, of a smoky chimney, these will all admit of remedy or, at least, will last only for a time, while by imparting wrong ideas to a child you not only injure this child but the errors are transmitted to posterity. It is better to make one thousand machines wrong, then to train up a child as he should not go. No person should take up the business because it is less repulsive or because it is more honorable, or easier or more advantageous in a pecuniary view. The question to be asked is, how the best good can be obtained by others & not ourselves.

It should be regarded as a sacred office, to be approached only with a desire to do good. He must have a conviction that it is the way in which he may do the most good. He should feel a deep interest in his scholars, & a love for his business.—Those whose object is to get money, or to pass away time, should be advised to turn their attention to another profession.—There are certain qualities which are very desirable to a teacher—not that he intended to say they were indispensible, but that they were very great additions. The 1st is Health—some leave other occupations as too laborious and teach a school, thinking that the trials of the school room are much less than those of any other station. Health is essential to the teacher, not only on his own account but for the sake of his pupils. To the sick, every trial is doubled.—Some suffering bad health are better teachers, than those enjoying good, but if the same person were possessed with health, he would be probably a much better teacher.—Personal deformity would be an objection not but that a dwarf or cripple *may* keep a better school than one formed with most perfect symmetry, but it would be better that the children should have the beauties of nature presented to them, than the deformities. 2nd a fair reputation and good standing in community. If people speak slightily *(sic)* of you in the town in which you have a school, you will find your scholars will disrespect you.—4th, a well balanced mind, free from eccentricities & from the infirmities of genius.—A person may have too much, as well as too little genius for a teacher.—5th a deep interest in children—she must feel an interest in whatever interests them; in their joys & their sorrows. Children readily perceive those who are interested in them, & feel hurt by coldness. 6th Patience, mildness, firmness, & perfect self control, are essential properties to every teacher. Patience is requisite to meet the various trials which will beset you. You may not make so much impression by mildness in one instance, but in the end, much more will be accomplished. Mildness in manner, measures, language, countenance & in every thing else.

Firmness is especially necessary, be firm to your plans;

let your measures be the same each day—A teacher without these virtues, may be compared to a city without walls; which the enemy enters without opposition, & does what he chooses after entering. 7th nice moral discrimination, a high sense of moral responsibility, & accountability—The knowledge that you are accountable to a being superior to man, sustains you.—Teachers should be acquainted with their difficulties, and know how to surmount them. The government should be just, uniform, & impartial. All rules should be made so that the pupils can see they are for their good, & the reasons for making them should be explained. Teachers should be well acquainted with the branches they are to teach.— The next lecture will be upon the responsibilities of a teacher & School order & government.—

CYRUS PEIRCE TO HENRY BARNARD*
(1841)

You ask for a full account of my manner of instruction in the *art of Teaching*. This it is not easy to give. From what I say, you may get some idea of what I *attempt*, and of the *manner* of it. Two things I have aimed at, especially in this school. 1. To teach *thoroughly* the principles of the several branches studied, so that the pupils may have a *clear* and *full understanding* of them. 2. To teach the pupils, by my own *example*, as well as by *precepts*, the *best way of teaching the same things* effectually to others. I have four different methods of recitation. 1st, by question and answer; 2d, by conversation; 3d, by calling on one, two, three, more or less, to give an analysis of the whole subject contained in the lesson;

* *The First State Normal School in America,* pp. l–liii.

and 4th, by requiring written analyses, in which the *ideas* of the author are stated in the *language* of the pupil. I do not mean that these are all practised at the same exercise. The students understand that, at all the recitations, they are at perfect liberty to suggest queries, doubts, opinions. At all the recitations we have more or less of discussion. Much attention is paid to the *manner* in which the pupils *set forth, or state* their positions. I am ever mingling, or attempting to mingle, at these exercises, theory and example; frequently putting the inquiry to them, not only, "How do you understand such and such a statement?" but, "How would you express such and such a sentiment, or explain such a principle, or illustrate such a position to a class, which you may be teaching?" "Let me," I say to them, "hear your statements, or witness your modes of illustrating and explaining." In this connection, I frequently call them to the black-board for visible representation. They make the attempt; I remark upon their manner of doing it, and endeavor to show them in what respect it may be improved. Sometimes, instead of reciting the lesson directly to me, I ask them to imagine themselves, for the time, acting in the *capacity* of *teachers,* to a class of young pupils, and to adopt a style suitable for such a purpose. At many of our recitations, more than half the time is spent with reference to teaching *"the art of teaching."* Besides delivering to the school a written *Formal Lecture* once a week, in which I speak of the qualifications, motives, and duties of teachers, the discipline, management, and instruction of schools, and the *manner* in which the various branches should be taught, I am every day, in conversations, or a familiar sort of lectures, taking up and discussing more *particularly* and *minutely,* some point or points suggested by the exercises or occurrences, it may be, of the day, relating to the *internal operations* of the schoolroom, or to physical, moral, or intellectual education:—I say much about the views and motives of teachers, and the motives by which they should attempt to stimulate their pupils. And here I would state, that my theory goes to the entire exclusion of the *premium and emulation system,* and of corporal punishment. My confidence in it is sustained and strengthened by a full and fair experiment for more than one year in a public school composed of seventy scholars of both sexes. I am constantly calling-up real or supposed cases, and either asking the pupils what they would do, in such case, or stating to them what I would do myself, or both. As a specimen of such questions, take the following, viz: On going into a school as teacher, what is the first thing you would do? How will you proceed to bring to order, and arrange your school? Will you have many rules, or few? Will you announce beforehand a code of laws, or make special rules as they may be needed? What *motives* do you purpose to appeal to, and what *means* will you adopt to make your pupils interested in their studies? What method will you adopt to teach spelling, reading, arithmetic? What will you do with the perseveringly idle and troublesome? What will you do if your scholars quarrel? lie? swear? What will you do if a scholar tells you he *won't* do as he is directed? If a question in any ordinary lesson, say arithmetic, comes up, which you cannot solve readily, what will be your resort? Should you be chiefly ambitious to teach *much,* or to teach thoroughly? How would you satisfy yourself that your teaching is thorough, effectual? To what branches shall you attach most importance, and why? Will you aim chiefly to exercise the *faculties,* or communicate instruction? Besides these daily discussions or conversations, we have a *regular debate* every Saturday, in which the principles involved in these and similar questions are discussed.

Reading I teach by oral inculcation of the principles, as contained in Porter's Rhetorical Reader, (which strike me as in the main correct,) and by example, reading myself before the whole class; hearing the pupils read, and then reading the same piece myself, pointing out their faults, and calling upon them to read again and again, and even the third and fourth time. They also read to each other in my presence. This is a most difficult art to teach. Very few good teachers are to be found, either in our schools or elsewhere. Spelling I teach both orally and by *writing* from the reading lesson; for I think each method has its advantages. Orthography has not yet received quite its merited attention in our schools. *Most* persons in business life have to *write;* few, comparatively, are called upon to read publicly; for this reason it is more important to be a correct speller than a fine reader.

I have adopted no text-book in teaching geography. Worcester's is *chiefly* used. My method has been to give out a subject, (a particular country, e.g.,) for examination. The class make search, using what maps and books they have at command, and get all the information of every kind they can, statistical, historical, geographical, of the people, manners, religion, government, business, etc., and at the recitation we have the *results* of their researches. Giving to each a separate subject, I sometimes require the pupils to make an imaginary voyage, or journey, to one, two, three, or more countries, and give an account of every thing on their return. If I were to teach geography to a class of *young beginners,* I should commence with the town in which they live.

In grammar I have adopted no particular text-book.

I am teaching a class of beginners in the model school without a book.

In moral instruction we use both Wayland and Combe; and our recitations are conducted as above described. There are no subjects in which scholars manifest more interest than in questions of morals. This I have noticed in all schools. It shows how easy it would be to do what is so much needed, if the teachers are disposed; viz., to cultivate the *moral faculties*. In connection with reading the Scriptures at the opening of the school in the morning, it is my practice to remark on points of practical duty, as far as I can go on common ground.

10. *Annexed school, or model school.*—This school consists of thirty pupils, of both sexes, from the age of six to ten, inclusive, taken promiscuously from families in the various districts of the town. The children pay nothing for tuition; find their own books, and bear the incidental expenses. This school is under the general superintendence and inspection of the Principal of the Normal School. After it was arranged, the general course of instruction and discipline being settled, it was committed to the immediate care of the pupils of the Normal School, one acting as superintendent, and two as assistants, for one month in rotation, for all who are thought prepared to take a part in its instruction. In this experimental school, the teachers are expected to apply the principles and methods which they have been taught in the Normal School, with liberty to suggest any improvements, which may occur to them. Twice every day the Principal of the Normal School goes into the model school for general observation and direction, spending from one half to one hour each visit.

CYRUS PEIRCE TO HENRY BARNARD*
(1851)

DEAR SIR:—You ask me "what I aimed to accomplish, and would aim to accomplish now, with my past experience before me, in a Normal School."

I answer briefly, that it was my aim, and it would be my aim again, to make better teachers, and especially, better teachers for our common schools; so that those primary seminaries, on which so many depend for their education, might answer, in a higher degree, the end of their institution. Yes, to make better teachers; teachers who would understand, and do their business better; teachers, who should know more of the nature of children, of youthful developments, more of the subjects to be taught, and more of the true methods of teaching; who would teach more philosophically, more in harmony with the natural development of the young mind, with a truer regard to the order and connection in which the different branches of knowledge should be presented to it, and, of course, more successfully.

Again, I felt that there was a call for a truer government, a higher training and discipline, in our schools; that the appeal to the rod, to a sense of shame and fear of bodily pain, so prevalent in them, had a tendency to make children mean, secretive, and vengeful, instead of high-minded, truthful, and generous; and I wished to see them in the hands of teachers, who could understand the higher and purer motives of action, as gratitude, generous affection, sense of duty, by which children should be influenced, and under which their whole character should be formed.

In short, I was desirous of putting our schools into the

* *The First State Normal School in America*, pp. 278–285.

hands of those who would make them places in which children could learn, not only to read, and write, and spell, and cipher, but gain information on various other topics, (as accounts, civil institutions, natural history, physiology, political economy, &c.) which would be useful to them in after life, and have all their faculties, (physical, intellectual and moral) trained in such harmony and proportion, as would result in the highest formation of character. This is what I supposed the object of Normal Schools to be. Such was my object.

[*Do teachers need training?*]

But in accepting the charge of the first American Institution of this kind, I did not act in the belief that there were no good teachers, or good schools among us; or that I was more wise, more fit to teach, than all my fellows. On the contrary, I knew that there were, both within and without Massachusetts, excellent schools, and not a few of them, and teachers wiser than myself; yet my conviction was strong, that the ratio of such schools to the whole number of schools were small; and that the teachers in them, for the most part, had grown up to be what they were, from long observation, and through the discipline of an experience painful to themselves, and more painful to their pupils.

It was my impression also, that a majority of those engaged in school-keeping, taught few branches, and those imperfectly, that they possessed little fitness for their business, did not understand well, either the nature of children or the subjects they professed to teach, and had little skill in the art of teaching or governing schools. I could not think it possible for them, therefore, to make their instructions very intelligible, interesting, or profitable to their pupils, or present to them the motives best

Cyrus Peirce and Mary Swift

adapted to secure good lessons and good conduct, or, in a word, adopt such a course of training as would result in a sound development of the faculties, and the sure formation of a good character.

I admitted that a skill and power to do all this might be acquired by trial, if teachers continued in their business long enough; but while teachers were thus learning, I was sure that pupils must be suffering. In the process of time, a man may find out by experiment, (trial), how to tan hides and convert them into leather. But most likely the time would be long, and he would spoil many before he got through. It would be far better for him, we know, to get some knowledge of Chemistry, and spend a little time in his neighbor's tannery, before he sets up for himself. In the same way the farmer may learn what trees, and fruits, and seeds, are best suited to particular soils, and climates, and modes of culture, but it must be by a needless outlay of time and labor, and the incurring of much loss. If wise, he would first learn the principles and facts which agricultural experiments have already established, and then commence operations. So the more I considered the subject, the more the conviction grew upon my mind, that by a judicious course of study, and of discipline, teachers may be prepared to enter on their work, not only with the hope, but almost with the assurance of success.

[*Are there principles of education?*]

I did not then, I do not now, (at least in the fullest extent of it,) assent to the doctrine so often expressed in one form or another, that there are no general principles to be recognized in education; no general methods to be followed in the art of teaching; that all depends upon the individual teacher; that every principle, motive and method, must owe its power to the skill with which it is applied; that what is true, and good, and useful in the hands of one, may be quite the reverse in the hands of another; and of course, that every man must invent his own methods of teaching and governing, it being impossible successfully to adopt those of another. To me it seemed that education had claims to be regarded as a science, being based on immutable principles, of which the practical teacher, though he may modify them to meet the change of ever-varying circumstances, can never lose sight.

[*What are these principles?*]

That the educator should watch the operations of nature, the development of the mind, discipline those faculties whose activities first appear, and teach that knowledge first, which the child can most easily comprehend, viz., that which comes in through the senses, rather than through reason and the imagination; that true education demands, or rather implies the training, strengthening, and perfecting of all the faculties by means of the especial exercise of each; that in teaching, we must begin with what is simple and known, and go on by easy steps to what is complex and unknown; that for true progress and lasting results, it were better for the attention to be concentrated on a few studies, and for a considerable time, than to be divided among many, changing from one to another at short intervals; that in training children we must concede a special recognition to the principle of curiosity, a love of knowledge, and so present truth as to keep this principle in proper action; that the pleasure of acquiring, and the advantage of possessing knowledge, may be made, and should be made, a sufficient stimulus to sustain wholesome exertion without resorting to emulation, or medals, or any rewards other than those which are the natural fruits of industry and attainment; that for securing order and obedience, there are better ways than to depend solely or chiefly upon the rod, or appeals to fear; that much may be done by way of prevention of evil; that gentle means should always first be tried; that undue attention is given to intellectual training in our schools, to the neglect of physical and moral; that the training of the faculties is more important than the communication of knowledge; that the discipline, the instruction of the school-room, should better subserve the interests of real life, than it now does;—these are some of the principles, truths, facts, in education, susceptible, I think, of the clearest demonstration, and pretty generally admitted now, by all enlightened educators.

[*The principles of teaching suggest reform of the old methods of teaching the common branches.*]

The old method of teaching Arithmetic, for instance, by taking up some printed treatise and solving abstract questions consisting of large numbers, working blindly by what must appear to the pupil arbitrary rules, would now be regarded as less philosophical, less in conformity to mental development, than the more modern way of beginning with mental Arithmetic, using practical questions, which involve small numbers, and explaining the reason of every step as you go along.

So in the study of Grammar, no Normal teacher, whether a graduate or not, of a Normal School, would require his pupils to commit the whole text-book to memory, before looking at the nature of words, and their application in the structure of sentences. Almost all have found out that memorizing the Grammar-book, and the exercise of parsing, do very little toward giving one a knowledge of the English language.

Neither is it learning Geography, to read over and commit to memory, statistics of the length and breadth of countries, their boundaries, latitude and longitude, &c., &c., without map or globe, or any visible illustration, as was once the practice. Nor does the somewhat modern addition of maps and globes much help the process, unless the scholar, by a previous acquaintance with objects in the outer world, has been prepared to use them. The shading for mountains, and black lines for rivers on maps, will be of little use to a child who has not already some idea of a mountain and a river.

And the teacher who should attempt to teach reading by requiring a child to repeat from day to day, and from month to month, the whole alphabet, until he is familiar with all the letters, as was the fashion in former days, would deserve to lose his place and be sent himself to school. Could anything be more injudicious? Is it not more in harmony with nature's work, to begin with simple, significant words, or rather sentences, taking care always to select such as are easy and intelligible, as well as short? Or, if letters be taken first, should they not be formed into small groups, on some principle of association, and be combined with some visible object?

Surely, the different methods of teaching the branches above-mentioned, are not all equally good. Teaching is based on immutable principles, and may be regarded as an art.

[*How Peirce attempted to teach the art of teaching.*]

Nearly thirty years' experience in the business of teaching, I thought, had given me some acquaintance with its true principles and processes, and I deemed it no pre-

Cyrus Peirce and Mary Swift

sumption to believe that I could teach them to others. This I attempted to do in the Normal School at Lexington; 1st. didactically, i.e. by precept, in the form of familiar conversations and lectures; 2nd. by giving every day, and continually, in my own manner of teaching, an exemplification of my theory; 3rd. by requiring my pupils to teach each other in my presence, the things which I had taught them; and 4th. by means of the Model School, where, under my general supervision, the Normal pupils had an opportunity, both to prove and improve their skill in teaching and managing schools. At all our recitations, (the modes of which were very various,) and in other connections, there was allowed the greatest freedom of inquiry and remark, and principles, modes, processes, every thing indeed relating to schoolkeeping, was discussed. The thoughts and opinions of each one were thus made the property of the whole, and there was infused into all hearts a deeper and deeper interest in the teachers' calling. In this way the Normal School became a kind of standing Teachers' Institute.

But for a particular account of my manner and processes at the Normal School, allow me to refer you to a letter which I had the honor, at your request, to address to you from Lexington, Jan. 1, 1841, and which was published in the Common School Journal, both of Connecticut and Massachusetts, (vol. 3.)

What success attended my labors, I must leave to others to say. I acknowledge, it was far from being satisfactory to myself. Still the experiment convinced me that Normal Schools may be made a powerful auxiliary to the cause of education. A thorough training in them, I am persuaded, will do much toward supplying the want of experience. It will make the teachers' work easier, surer, better. I have reason to believe that Normal pupils are much indebted for whatever of fitness they possess for teaching, to the Normal School. They uniformly profess so to feel. I have, moreover, made diligent inquiry in regard to their success, and it is no exaggeration to say, that it has been manifestly great. Strong testimonials to the success of many of the early graduates of the Lexington (now W. Newton) Normal School, were published with the 8th Report of the late Secretary of the Board of Education, and may be found in the 7th vol. of the Massachusetts Common School Journal.

[*Do we need professional schools for teachers?*]

But it is sometimes asked, (and the inquiry deserves an answer,) Allowing that teaching is an art, and that teachers may be trained for their business, have we not High Schools and Academies, in which the various school branches are well taught? May not teachers in them be prepared for their work? Where is the need then of a distinct order of Seminaries for training teachers? I admit we have Academies, High Schools, and other schools, furnished with competent teachers, in which is excellent teaching; but at the time of the establishment of the Normal Schools in Massachusetts, there was not, to my knowledge, any first-rate institution exclusively devoted to training teachers for our common schools; neither do I think there is now any, except the Normal Schools. And teachers can not be prepared for their work anywhere else, so well as in seminaries exclusively devoted to this object. The art of teaching must be made the great, the paramount, the only concern. It must not come in as subservient to, or merely collateral with any thing else whatever. And again, a Teachers' Seminary should have annexed to it, or rather as an integral part of it, a model, or experimental school for practice.

Were I to be placed in a Normal School again, the only

difference in my aim would be to give more attention to the development of the faculties, to the spirit and motives by which a teacher should be moved, to physical and moral education, to the inculcation of good principles and good manners.

[*Conclusion: What the professionally-trained teacher should be able to do.*]

In conclusion, allow me to recapitulate. It was my aim, and it would be my aim again, in a Normal School, to raise up for our common schools especially, a better class of teachers,—teachers who would not only teach more and better than those already in the field, but who would govern better; teachers, who would teach in harmony with the laws of juvenile development, who would secure diligent study and good lessons and sure progress, without a resort to emulation and premiums, and good order from higher motives than the fear of the rod or bodily pain; teachers, who could not only instruct well in the common branches, as reading, writing, arithmetic, &c., but give valuable information on a variety of topics, such as accounts, history, civil institutions, political economy, and physiology; bring into action the various powers of children, and prepare them for the duties of practical life; teachers, whose whole influence on their pupils, direct and indirect, should be good, tending to make them, not only good readers, geographers, grammarians, arithmeticians, &c., but good scholars, good children, obedient, kind, respectful, mannerly, truthful; and in due time, virtuous, useful citizens, kind neighbors, high-minded, noble, pious men and women. And this I attempted to do by inculcating the truth in the art of teaching and governing,—the truth in all things; and by giving them a living example of it in my own practice.

[CYRUS PEIRCE]

2. Richard Edwards: "Normal Schools in the United States"*
(1865)

When those attending the first American normal-school convention in 1859 passed a resolution declaring that "education is a science," Richard Edwards protested in vain. He argued that sciences are built by research and not by proclamation. One is tempted here to digress: the protests of men like Edwards have been too long ignored by educators who believe that passing a resolution in solemn convention makes of a hope a fact. But Edwards' argument is cited simply as evidence that he was among the more tough-minded early normal-school leaders.

Edwards had been a student of Nicholas Tillinghast at the Bridgewater (Massachusetts) Normal School, and Tillinghast had been the only one of Horace Mann's early normal-school principals to resist the Massachusetts policy of keeping secondary-school and collegiate subject matter (except mental and moral philosophy, which were thought to contain the "science of teaching") out of the normal-school curriculum. It is not surprising, then, that when Edwards became president of the new Illinois Normal University, he took the lead in making it an institution of collegiate level. Illinois Normal University became one of the first and greatest "teachers colleges" and led the transformation of the

* National Teachers' Association, *Lectures and Proceedings, 1865*, pp. 277–282.

normal schools from institutions of secondary-school level to institutions of higher education. It was from Illinois Normal that the first band of American teacher-educators went to study at the German universities, from which they returned with Herbartian psychology and pedagogy.

Edwards was neither maudlin sentimentalist nor anti-intellectual, though there were a number of both in the early normal-school movement. Had he been of this number, one could more easily discount his commitment to the single-purpose teacher education institution. In the third and fourth decades of the twentieth century, one still heard his commitment echoed by those who considered the "teachers college slant" important. In the seventh decade, their voices are barely audible, and the kind of institution they supported has virtually disappeared.

In large multi-purpose colleges and universities, potential teachers are lured into other professions, and one senses that those who do become teachers are less motivated by altruism, less "called" to serve than those prepared in single-purpose institutions. No doubt there are excellent reasons for the passing of the teachers college, but one must note, for example, that the science departments of the great universities produce but a handful of people prepared and willing to teach science in the secondary school. There was loss as well as gain in the passing of institutions the beginning and end of whose purpose was the preparation of good elementary- and secondary-school teachers.

We say, then, most emphatically, that Normal Schools, with their distinctive characteristics, should be established and maintained in each State at public expense.

And what are these distinctive characteristics? Wherein and how does a Normal School differ from any other well-conducted institution, in which the same subjects in the main are taught?

First, we answer, it differs in its aim. Using, to a great extent, the same instruments as other schools, namely, treatises upon science and language, it nevertheless uses them for purposes very diverse. In an ordinary school, the treatise on arithmetic is put into the hands of the student in order that he may *learn arithmetic;* in the Normal School, the same book is used to enable him to learn *how to teach* arithmetic. In the ordinary school, the youth reads his Cicero with the purpose of learning the structure, vocabulary, and power of the Latin language; the normal student pores over the same author that he may adjust in his mind a method by which he may most successfully teach others these things. Both use the same materials, acquire, to some extent, the same knowledge, but aiming all the while at different ends. Of course it is clear that one of these objects must pre-suppose the accomplishment of the other. The proper work of the Normal School can not be performed unless the mastery of the subjects has first been obtained.

Because different men have to do with the same object, it does not follow that the sight or thought of it gives rise in their minds to the same associations. To the outward eye of the shipwright and sailor, the gallant ship, trim and taut, with canvas spread, and filled by the friendly breeze, is the same. To both she is an object of pride and admiration, but how different the scenes and duties of which she reminds the two! To one she recalls the shipyard with all its belongings—the stocks, the unwrought materials, the weary mortising, sawing, hammering, bolt-driving, caulking, and paying. He sees her as she was in the process of combination, while as yet her symmetry was undeveloped, and her beauty of line and curve existed only in the brain of the master-builder. To the other, she is a reminder of winds and waves, of distant voyages and foreign climes, of lonely watches and beating storms, of the midnight upon the glassy ocean and under the star-decked heavens. To the builder, she is, in an important sense, an end; his chief concern with her ceases when, for the first time, her sails filled, she glides, obedient to the helm, over the watery highway. To the mariner, she is a means, bearing him up amid the storm, protecting him against the dangers of the deep, gathering up for him the "wealth of Ormus and of Ind."

So with the subjects of study in school. To the ordinary student, arithmetic is associated, it may be, with severe efforts at mastering its principles; with perseverance and success, or irresolution and failure. But to him who is preparing to teach, it recalls the points most difficult of *explanation,* and the minds most difficult to reach. His constant question is, not "How can I master this principle or process?" but "How will this point seem to my pupils?" To one it is an end. His concern with it ceases when, obedient to his will, its principles come at call, and appear before his mind luminous and clear. To the other, it is a means to the training of mind. It is not enough for him that his eye can take in the whole field and scan the relation of the parts. He must see that, as an instrument, it does the work—accomplishes the result set for it. To him the study must culminate in an increase of intellectual and moral power somewhere. He must see, as the result of it all, a well-developed, symmetrical, human soul!

In these schools the whole animus of both teacher and

pupil is this idea of future teaching. Every plan is made to conform to it. Every measure proposed is tried by this as a test. There is no other aim or purpose to claim any share of the mental energy of either. It is the Alpha and Omega of schemes of study and modes of thought.

And is this distinct and separate aim in the preparatory seminary of any value to the novice? Will he be likely, on account of this, to make a better teacher than he would without it—his training, in all other respects, being the same? In answer to this question we say, most emphatically, Yes! And in so saying we doubtless express the conviction of every educator who has given the subject much thought. May we not say that if every scrap of educational literature were to be blotted out; if Comenius were to be forgotten with all his works; if Roger Ascham were to fade out from the literary horizon; if Pestalozzi were to become as a myth; if the educational utterances of Socrates, Plato, and Quintilian were to be eliminated from the sun of human knowledge; if Horace Mann, with the thoughts and the inspiration he has left us, were to vanish from book and from memory; if all this were to happen, and if nothing were to be left the teacher and pupil in the Normal School but their own thought and their unaided efforts, may we not even then say that these institutions, by the mere force of the fact that their aim is what it is, would be not only useful but necessary —ay, all the more necessary on account of these very circumstances? Shall we not, therefore, concede that the difference in aim between the normal and ordinary school makes one of the distinctive and essential characteristics of the former, and that this difference is of itself sufficient to establish its claim to separate support?

But thank God, the wise utterances of the past are still with us. Pestalozzi has not faded out. Horace Mann is commemorated not alone or chiefly in statue and monument, however honorable these may be to those who rear them. Literature preserves for us the results of ancient and modern thought and experience on the subject of education. And the Normal School has, therefore, for one of its distinctive characteristics, that it imparts instruction in the science of education and the art of teaching. Thoughtful men have observed the phenomena of the mind, juvenile and adult, have compared the results of their observations, and have given us the truths and principles evolved by their thinking. These we are able, to some extent, to present to our normal students, as helps in forming their own opinions, and constructing their own theories of education. And every year improves the material thus furnished. In our times many able minds are intensely laboring upon this problem of ascertaining and stating the principles of education. Books are continually issuing from the press setting them forth. Of course, in the multiplicity of publications, there has been some trash. In our eagerness we have plucked some immature fruit. The tree is young and has not yet, we are confident, reached its best bearing. But already some plump and lucious specimens have fallen into our baskets. And we know that more and finer is yet to come. In the meantime let us cherish the tree. Let the soil be tilled by the assiduous labor of every active teacher. Let it be watered by the generous showers of a beneficent legislation; and let it be warmed into lusty life and a glorious fruitage by the genial rays of an appreciative public sentiment!

It has been sometimes intimated that this pretended science of education is a myth—that the talk about it is of little account. It has been charged, perhaps not altogether generously, that its advocates and professors are more enthusiastic than wise—that they are either intentional deceivers of the public, or unwitting deceivers of themselves—that, in short, the whole matter is a sort of well-intentioned imposture. Now we are free to confess that some of the talk aforesaid has been a trifle unsubstantial—that an occasional apostle has appeared with more zeal than knowledge—that some of the professors, it is barely possible, have chipped the shell a little prematurely. But it is not, I trust, necessary, at this late day, to assure you that there is here as noble a science as ever engaged the thought of man. There are immutable principles here, that ought to be studied and comprehended by every young person entering upon the work of teaching. There is, in the nature of things, a foundation for a profession of teachers. Compare the science of education with other sciences in this respect. Take the science of Medicine. Have we not well-defined, universally acknowledged, practically important principles as well in the Teachers' College as the College of Physicians? and as the science of medicine now is, with its various schools and numerous isms, have we not about as many of them that are universally acknowledged? Or take the clerical profession, including all the denominations considered respectable, and are there not as many useful and important points, upon which we teachers are all agreed, as there are among the ministers? In truth, the science of education is now, in some respects, in the most satisfactory condition. It conclusions have not crystallized into such rigid forms that there is no room for further discussion. Its principles are sufficiently well-established to serve as guides to the thoughtful inquirer, but not sufficiently limited to cramp his faculties or repress his thought.

Here then we have the second distinctive characteristic

of the Normal School—that it instructs its pupils in the Science of Education and Art of Teaching.

Another essential requisite in a Normal School is, that it gives its pupils an opportunity of some kind for practice in teaching, under the supervision and subject to the criticism of experienced and skillful instructors. This is accomplished in various ways; by exercises in conducting the regular classes of the Normal School; by classes of normal pupils assuming for the time the character of children, and receiving instruction and answering questions as they think children would; and by a separate school of children in which the novice is intrusted with the charge of a class, either permanently or for a stated period, as a week or two weeks, as the case may be. There seem to be different opinions as to which of these is the best and most efficient method. The Model or Experimental School has been objected to because it interferes with the daily drill of the normal student in his classes, and also because the children taught by these students are supposed not to be so well taught as they would be by instructors of more experience. But I think both these evils may be entirely avoided—the first, by a proper distribution of the time for study and for teaching, and the second, by an adequate supervision of the pupil-teachers, added to the responsibility imposed upon them by continuing the same class, under the same teacher, during a term of school, and subjecting it at the close of that term to such an examination as is usual in the case of regular teachers. The school for practice is unquestionably essential to the complete idea of a Normal School. When the young practitioner is dealing with children, he encounters the reality of his work. The actual difficulties of his employment are before him. There is no make-believe. He is never in doubt as to whether his methods are such as to instruct and interest children, for the children are there, and he can see for himself, and all others can do the same, whether they are instructed and interested, or not. Every question he asks, every suggestion he makes, is tested on the spot by the proper and natural test. But it is said that more skill is necessary to teach a class of adults personating children, than to teach an equal number of actual little ones, and that, therefore, this practice is of more value than the other. This statement may be true in respect to the difficulty, and if we knew that every additional degree of difficulty adds strength to the mind overcoming it, we might allow that higher results might be gained in this way than by the other. But this assumption is not true. It is more difficult to calculate an eclipse than to ascertain the value of ten pounds of sugar at twenty cents a pound, and what a vast increase of mental strength is acquired in passing from the latter to the former. But it is also more difficult to shoot pigeons with a sixty-four pounder than with a common fowling-piece, and most difficult of all to see any advantage that is likely to come from the attempt. Increasing the difficulty of an undertaking does not necessarily improve its effect. Unnatural methods of accomplishing results are difficult, and certainly not to be commended on that or any other account.

Again we mention as a distinctive characteristic of Normal Schools that they beget an *esprit du corps,* and kindle a glowing enthusiasm among their pupils. They tend to exalt the business of teaching. They show it up in its nobler instead of its meaner colors. By infusing an element of philosophy into the very work of instruction, they dignify every step of it. Under this influence the work of primary instruction becomes the worthiest of the whole task, because, considered with respect to the child's wants, it is the most important. It takes profounder insight into the child's nature to lay aright the foundations of his culture in the primary school, than to help him at any other stage of his progress, because the primary teacher must see the end from the very beginning. His plans for the future must embrace the child's entire career. No partial view of the field is sufficient. This the Normal School brings into view and insists upon. Admit this truth and you at once exalt the work of elementary instruction into a dignified science, into something worth the study of any mind. Make the excellence of teaching to depend upon *what* you teach, and there is little to arouse the enthusiasm of some of our number, for a knowledge of the alphabet and abs can hardly be considered as bestowing much dignity on one.

Normal Schools, then, should be reëstablished and maintained by State authority. For this we urge the consideration that they are needed to promote the success of the common schools, and that they are eminently adapted to this purpose. This adaptation we have tried to prove from the distinguishing characteristics of these institutions. These characteristics are that they have in view the special object of preparing teachers, that this is their entire aim and end; that they foster a professional spirit and generate professional enthusiasm; that they give instruction in the science and art of teaching; and that just now, as our country is situated, they are specially needed, in order to extend the influence of free schools all over the region lately blasted by slavery. Any one of these characteristics is a sufficient vindication of these institutions. Taken together, they form an argument in behalf of normal schools irresistable and imposing. May these institutions continue to grow in usefulness and in public favor until they have achieved results worthy of the confidence they solicit.

3. College and University Responsibility for Teacher Education: Addresses to the New England Association of Colleges and Preparatory Schools (1888–1889)

There had been early and sporadic talk in New England about using the colleges for the professional instruction of teachers. The pressure in this direction had been eased, however, by the rise of the normal schools. The question was seriously reopened only when the growth of secondary-school attendance created a vastly greater demand for teachers and when education as a field of study began to find a place in the university curriculum. In the speech partially reproduced below, Charles Kendall Adams carried the issue to the floor of the New England Association of Colleges and Preparatory Schools.

It is significant that Adams based his case for the teaching of pedagogy in the colleges and universities largely on the assumption that secondary-school teachers must carry the burden of educational reform. Proposals for the university study of education were always accompanied by the argument that prospective teachers had to be prepared for educational leadership as well as pedagogical craftsmanship. The talented and liberally educated amateurs like Horace Mann had prescribed both curriculum and pedagogical method for the elementary-school teachers trained in the normal schools. But after the Civil War, educational leadership came increasingly to be viewed as a professional function, and the secondary-school teacher was most commonly expected to assume this function in his community. This expectation, as well as the traditional concern of college and university faculties with the more theoretical and scientific subjects, made university teacher education different from that provided in the normal schools.

At the meeting the year following the Adams speech, J. B. Sewall made the case for keeping the liberal arts college "pure." We have only the reporter's notes on the discussion that followed, a discussion in which Charles W. Eliot, G. Stanley Hall, and other distinguished New England college and university presidents participated. In general, these men were highly skeptical of the Adams position. Most of them accepted it "in principle" but expressed grave doubt that there was enough scientific knowledge of pedagogy to warrant the development of university courses in education. No one was more skeptical than Eliot, whose position is especially interesting in view of the fact that he had already invited G. Stanley Hall to give a series of lectures on pedagogy at Harvard and was shortly to appoint Paul Hanus as professor of education. Did he believe that the university should encourage the scientific study of education but not provide professional training for teachers? Was he in the process of changing his mind? Or did he simply ride with the tide of opinion? Perhaps he simply enjoyed the role of "devil's advocate."

CHARLES KENDALL ADAMS:
"THE TEACHING OF PEDAGOGY
IN COLLEGES AND UNIVERSITIES"*
(1888)

The importance of education reveals and determines the importance of the teacher's function. If it be true that there is no interest of the community that is more universal and far-reaching, then it must also be true that there is no vocation that has more to do with the real welfare of the people. If there is any pursuit upon the character of which the future of society, in any exceptional measure, depends, it is fit that those by whom the character of that profession is determined should be exceptionally well prepared for their work. It follows, as a necessary consequence, that the teacher should be trained with special thoroughness for his vocation.

From one point of view this would seem not to be necessary. The teacher in the course of his own training has had abundant opportunities for observing good and bad methods of instruction; and, so far as wisdom can be derived from mere observation, he would seem to have had the means of obtaining not a little knowledge of the art. It has to be admitted, of course, that the vocation of the teacher differs in this respect from almost, or quite every other vocation or pursuit. The lawyer and the physician when entering on the study of their respective professions have enjoyed no special facilities for observing the methods of successful practice. The training of the preacher is perhaps the only one that seems to present any very striking resemblances or analogies. But if the student who determines to go into the pulpit has usually had abundant opportunities for observing the methods of the

* New England Association of Colleges and Preparatory Schools, *Addresses and Proceedings, 1888*, pp. 17–19, 26–29.

successful preacher, it is nevertheless true that these opportunities do not, in the estimation of the public, exempt him from the necessity of a thorough professional training. No argument for such exemption on the part of the teacher can therefore be drawn from the analogous vocation of the pulpit.

Moreover, experience shows that mere observation is an unsafe guide. At best, observation can teach only the mere method of imparting instruction; whereas no small part of the vocation consists of knowing what to teach and what to leave untaught. Of this part of the work, great and important as it is, no pupil has any opportunity of learning anything by mere observation. It follows, therefore, that the untrained teacher is obliged to pick up at haphazard and by dint of observation, and perhaps long and painful experience, a knowledge of a very large part of the means and conditions of success.

It is not, of course, to be inferred from this that experience is not sometimes the most successful of teachers. Nor is it to be denied that the great and rare art of most successfully imparting instruction is a gift that seems often to have been bestowed by nature herself. And yet who has not observed that sometimes the most successful teachers have grown slowly into their exceptional efficiency by a painstaking experience leading them gradually away from a most unpromising beginning? It would be flying in the face of all observation and experience to deny that many of the best teachers have come up to their present condition with no other helps than the gifts of nature and opportunity; but this important fact no more proves the inutility of training than the successes of Washington and Franklin and Lincoln prove the inutility of a collegiate education. We must, in judging of every subject of this kind, eliminate the exceptional examples of genius, and form our opinions from results on the great uninspired masses of mankind. Let us, then, apply this method, and ascertain, if possible, whether the experience of others has anything of importance to show us. Let us put to such tests as we can command, the two methods to which I refer. Let us compare the results of the two methods as they reveal themselves in the two countries where they have been most thoroughly tried. In doing so, we shall have to place definitely before our minds what has been done in the two countries selected; and then, as best we can, we must compare the results of the efforts that have been made. Let us take for comparison our own country on the one hand, and Prussia on the other. Prussia is selected, not because its methods are essentially different from those of other European states; —for, in the other German states, in Switzerland, in Sweden, even in France, the primary and secondary schools have been organized and developed on essentially the same plan—but because Prussia was the nation to devise the system; and because it is in Prussia, consequently, that the system has most perfectly borne its legitimate fruit. . . .[1]

I have thus endeavored to place the two classes of public schools sharply in contrast, in order that we may fully realize how inferior our schools really are. I am now speaking of the lower grades of schools; for I believe, as I have already said, that a comparison would not result in the same disadvantage to us if we carried it into the more advanced schools. But I believe that in the primary and lower grades no person of impartial judgment can observe our schools in comparison with those of Europe without admitting our great inferiority. We spend enor-

[1] In the deleted section, Adams contrasts the curriculum and teaching methods of Prussian schools for children from ages six to seventeen with those of American schools.—M. L. B.

mous sums in large and well-arranged school buildings and elegant furniture and expensive school books and then frustrate the purpose of them all by not having the one thing, compared with which, all the other things are as nothing, namely, A GOOD SCHOOL.

How is a change for the better to be brought about? In no other way than by a change of public opinion. This is, of course, the manner in which all reforms in a government like ours must proceed, and a radical change in this respect is absolutely necessary. There is in the public mind no general idea that our schools are inferior. Mr. Matthew Arnold, whose professional office it was to study educational systems, told the people of Europe in his report of 1868, that they had nothing to learn from American methods; and just after the Educational Exhibition in Philadelphia, in 1876, one of our oldest and wisest state superintendents declared that we had more to learn from Sweden and Russia in regard to methods of instruction than Sweden and Russia had to learn from us. But these were simply individual voices, and the prevailing belief in our country has been that, on the whole, so far from having any reason to be dissatisfied, we should be proud of our great and glorious system of free schools, and should abundantly thank God that we are not as other men are.

But then we may ask, in turn, How is this absurd popular optimism to be changed for the better? In no way, I answer, so readily, so rapidly, and so effectively, as by raising up and putting into positions of influence as large a class as possible of teachers who know what education is in those countries of the world where it has been most successful. And this brings me, after what I fear you will think a long wandering, to the subject of the systematic teaching of pedagogy in our schools and colleges.

In every college class there are certain ones who intend to be teachers; and as graduates from college they are to take positions to exert whatever influence can be exerted in behalf of the best educational methods. In all of our towns, it is, after all, the superintendents and teachers who exert the greatest influence in the formation of public opinion concerning our schools. It is, therefore, of great, I will say of unspeakable, importance, that this class of teachers should know what the world has to teach as to this art of teaching, which, as we have seen, in one country does so much, and in another does so little. It is certain, moreover, that much can be learned; for the study is not one of exceptional difficulty. The literature, especially in French and German, is abundant; and if this is well at the command of the teacher, there will be no difficulty in bringing to the class a mass of most valuable and helpful information.

Instruction in this subject, it seems to me, should consist of no less than four somewhat distinct parts; and these may well form four courses of instruction extending through the collegiate year. As to the order in which the student should take these courses, there may be some differences of opinion; but the courses themselves may be roughly described as follows:

1. The History of Education; ancient, medieval, and modern. While the enterprising teacher will depend chiefly upon lectures for giving life and inspiration to this course, some text-book, probably Compayré's "History of Pedagogy," should be required of the class at the recitations and examinations.

2. The Philosophy of Education. Analysis and discussion of the several theories that have prevailed, and that now prevail, in regard to the development of the human mind. This will involve, of course, a considera-

tion of the educational values of different studies, and of their effects on the growing mind. More psychological than any of the others, this course will depend for its success upon the philosophical bent and skill of the teacher. But the successful study and teaching of pedagogy, as a science, must rest very largely upon a psychological basis; and hence the best teachers have always laid considerable stress on this method. Paulsen, at Berlin, and Hall, at Johns Hopkins, were both teachers of philosophy as well as pedagogy in its more restricted sense. Payne, formerly of Michigan, but now of Tennessee, has given such a course with most satisfactory results.

3. Methods in the School Room. This is the practical side of the work, and should embrace a discussion of such questions as the art of teaching and governing; methods of most successfully imparting instruction; general school-room practice; general school management; the art of grading and arranging courses of study, and perhaps, the conducting of school institutes. This course, like the first, though dependent chiefly on the lectures of the Professor, should be accompanied with the careful use of some text-book, say Fitch's admirable "Lectures on Teaching."

4. The Teachers' Seminary. Here should be freely examined and discussed the most obscure and difficult problems that confront the teacher. A comparative study of educational systems may well form a part of the work here carried on. There should be the utmost freedom between Professor and student; indeed, in every respect, the meeting should have the informality of personal conference, rather than the formality of any approach to official relations.

Then, in addition to these courses, there may well be given by professors in the leading departments of the college or university courses designed exclusively to instruct how to teach young pupils the subject in hand. This is done in some of the universities of this country, as well as in many of the universities of Continental Europe. In the German universities it is carried not only into a theoretical discussion of what ought to be done, but also into the practical work of actual instruction. Some years ago I accompanied a class with Professor Masius, to one of the city schools of Leipzig, to witness an exercise of this kind. One of the Seminary students was put in charge of the class for the lesson of the hour, and the work was all done in the presence of the Professor and of the other members of the Seminary. Each of the members received practice of this kind, and the work of each was subjected to searching review and criticism by the other members and by the Professor, at the next meeting. The spirit of the exercise throughout was that of men who were putting the finishing touches to work in preparation for a profession of which they were proud, and to which their lives were henceforth with enthusiasm to be devoted. These, and such as these, are the men who teach the boys of Germany during all of the school days between nine and eighteen.

That in our own country we can at present have teachers thus trained and equipped to teach our boys during their grammar school days seems indeed too much to hope. Before that happy day comes, public opinion must undergo a revolution. But, until then, let us restrain all vain boasting; and, so far as is possible, bear ourselves with becoming humility. But in the meanwhile, be it long or be it short, what more promising method is there of changing public opinion than by the professional teaching of pedagogy in our colleges and universities?

J. B. SEWALL:
"THE DUTY OF THE COLLEGES TO MAKE PROVISION FOR THE TRAINING OF TEACHERS FOR SECONDARY SCHOOLS"*
(1889)

After the presentation made by President Adams last year, it is unnecessary to dwell upon the need of training on the part of the teacher of the Secondary School. It was made by him only too evident—I may say, painfully so, in view of the fact shown that so much is done in pedagogic for the German student who is to be a teacher, and that he enters, at least, upon his occupation so far in advance of the American secondary teacher. It remains for us to consider the duty of the colleges as regards the making provision for this training.

Let us begin by calling to mind what this training needed by the teacher of the Secondary School is.

It is twofold; first, the academic, that of a liberal education, which we may call the preparatory part, and second, the professional.

That the training of a liberal education is needed calls for no argument. The liberal education is that chiefly which gives the secondary teacher his equipment. It puts him in possession of the knowledge of what he is to teach, gives him some certain glimpse of its reaches and its touch with all other knowledge, has made him breathe the inspiring atmosphere of the world of thought and of thinkers of all time, and has exercised him in that discipline in which he is to exercise others. "A liberal education," one has said, (President Harris, *Congregationalist* Vol. 23 No. 18,) "awakens interest in knowledge, and its

* New England Association of Colleges and Preparatory Schools, *Addresses and Proceedings, 1889*, pp. 22–27.

acquisition and advancement, for its own sake, a large and liberal interest in all knowledge whether of nature or of man. It gives possession of the instruments of investigation, disciplines the man to concentration and persistence in work, developes and forms him, introduces him to the different departments of knowledge so that he appreciates the worth and relations of all, and unfolds the ability and disposition to prosecute literary or scientific pursuits as opportunity may offer through life." The liberal education, therefore, is the Secondary teacher's *sine qua non*. Indeed, from the mere fact that he is to stand at the threshold and open the door to the liberal education for others, it is impossible to conceive of him as equipped and disciplined for the service without it.

We come, then, to the professional training. What this is was also indicated by President Adams. There should be instruction in the History of Education, Ancient, Mediæval and Modern; in the Philosophy of Education, involving study of the mind as related to body, the development of mind, the value of different studies and their effects on the growing mind; in the Art of teaching, including the application of psychological principles and the use of methods; and practice in "The Teacher's Seminary," by which is meant the practice of free examination and discussion by teacher and pupils together of "all the most obscure and difficult problems which confront the teacher."

Is any argument needed to convince an intelligent mind that a training indicated by such a course of instruction is needed by the secondary teacher? Do not all teachers know from their own experience, that, so far as they have lacked this training at the outset, they have had slowly and laboriously to acquire it for themselves in the practice of their profession? It was from the fact that the

German teacher is provided with this course of training, —three years of professional training in the University followed by a rigid professional examination, and preceded by the nine years of gymnasial training—that the contrast between the American teacher and the German to the disadvantage of the former, was so clearly and disagreeably shown; that the work of teaching was more intelligently and thoroughly done, and with greater attainments at a given age on the part of the pupil than with us.

I pass, then, to the question before us.

If we ask, 'What are our colleges for?' we must answer, 'For the purpose of giving the liberal education.' The liberal education is preparatory to all the professions, and the college stands at the parting of the ways—the point whence the divergence of all the professional paths begins. This part of the duty then—to provide the liberal education—the colleges are for, they have taken it upon themselves, and it is required of them.

Is farther duty to be required of them as to pedagogic? I answer, qualifiedly, no. It being already their duty to provide the liberal education, they should not turn aside from or fall short of that aim. The secondary teacher, as we have seen, can require nothing less than the liberal education for his equipment; the intelligent parents of the boys who are to be put into his hands during the most plastic and formative period of life cannot be satisfied with anything less; the college must not give anything less. So far then as training in pedagogic is additional to the training in the liberal education, so far is it a handicap, and liable to infringe upon and diminish the liberal education. The college should no more take upon itself the burden of professional training in pedagogic than in law, medicine, or theology. Generally we should say that the college student who was taking up the study of medicine in his Senior year was diverting his attention from his proper course, and not deriving all the benefit he might and ought from the opportunities offered in the most important year of his course.

But the college does much in pedagogic incidentally, and my contention is, that when it has done its duty as a college, for liberal education, it has done its complete duty. What does it do incidentally?

1. It teaches the *to be* teacher how to work by making him work and by giving him examples of workers. Thus he learns by his own experience what to require of pupils, and how to make them render the work required. This supposes that his college professors are good teachers, not only themselves workers but knowing how to make him work. Good teachers are always stimulative and effective patterns. I have heard an eminent lawyer of this city speak in warmest terms of the strong influence exerted upon him when preparing for college, by two of his teachers, in the way of discipline, teaching how to work both by precept and example, and having the art of making him work. And Professor Sumner, of Yale, is quoted as saying that his teachers in the High School "employed in the school room all the best methods of teaching now so much gloried in, without apparently knowing that they had any peculiar method at all," and as often declaring in public that "as a teacher, he is deeply indebted to the sound traditions which he derived from these two men."—(*Popular Science Monthly*, June, 1889.)

But college professors are not always good teachers. There are often masters of particular departments of knowledge who are not masters of instruction. They can acquire but not impart. They can work themselves, but they can neither make others work, except by example, nor show them how to work. A great scholar may be, and very often is, a poor teacher, and it by no means holds good that a man who has obtained renown in a particular department is a good man to put into a professorial chair. But even in this case, there is not total absence of advantage. Men from under poor teachers have themselves become good teachers from a sense of their own wants in the pupil period and of the failures of their teachers to meet those wants. As the good teacher is a permanent object lesson, so is the poor. Men, remembering their own difficulties and needs, and how their teachers failed to see them, or if they saw them, failed to render any or the right kind of help, have successfully studied to be to their own pupils what their teachers were not to them. Perhaps each of us could name more than one teacher holding place in the foremost rank who has put himself there in this self-making way, with thanks— or no thanks—to his poor teachers.

The colleges then have performed their duty in making provision for the training of teachers for secondary schools when, first, they have opened the way and led their pupils over a course of study intelligently and wisely planned to the end of a liberal education: and second, when they have provided masters in instruction.

This as to colleges simple. We have colleges, however, which have grown or are growing into Universities, and with these as colleges I make the same contention, but as Universities the case is different. The University has taken upon itself the office, and therefore the duties corresponding, of opening lines and leading the way to different fields of attainment, some of culture and attainment only, others of practical use as professions. Harvard has a Divinity School, a Law School, a Scientific

School where one may study in preparation for being an Engineer, a Chemist, a Geologist, a Biologist, or an Electrical Engineer, a Medical School, a Dental School, a School of Veterinary Medicine, the Bussey Institution for Agriculture, and a graduate department in which the lines of study begun in the undergraduate course may be farther prosecuted, but no provision for instruction in the science and art of teaching. Why not? Teaching has now become a profession. Why ought not the University to make provision for it as much as for business, journalism or agriculture? Should not the same call which makes it a duty in any wise to provide these courses, make it a duty to provide a course in preparation for teaching? Is teaching less important than business or farming?

The same question might be asked of Yale, which makes provision for instruction in eight post-graduate courses, but not in pedagogic.

Columbia, Cornell, Michigan and the new Clark University happily do make the provision. Johns Hopkins did, but with the departure of Professor Stanley Hall to assume the presidency of Clark—Professor Hall gave there a special course in pedagogic—no formal instruction of that character has been given. Columbia gives one hour weekly through one year, intended as a post-graduate course, but open to seniors as an elective. Cornell makes the provision by lectures, discussions, and essays, open to juniors, seniors, and graduates. Michigan offers a course through two Semesters, by recitations, lectures, and the Seminarium, in arts and methods, school hygiene, school law, history of education, ancient, mediaeval, and modern school supervision, the principles underlying the arts of teaching and governing, the comparative study of educational systems, domestic and foreign, and in the Seminary, the study and discussion of special topics in the history and philosophy of education, and confers a teacher's Diploma upon students and post-graduates at the time they receive their Bachelor's or Master's degrees, provided certain prescribed studies have been pursued. Clark announces that President Hall "will direct the work of a few special students, not candidates for a degree, in the history, methods, and organization of education, elementary, intermediate, and superior. On these topics he will give a special course of lectures during a part of the year."

Thus it appears that our Universities, in part, have felt the duty of providing for the training of teachers, and have acknowledged it by making the provision in a degree. In this we will rejoice. But it also appears how small the provision is in comparison with that made by the German Universities, so that we are compelled to look upon it only as a beginning, and will hope and look for a large and strong development in this direction as rapidly as is possible.

4. Josiah Royce: "Is There a Science of Education?"* (1891)

When Paul Hanus moved to Harvard to occupy that university's first chair of pedagogy, philosopher Josiah Royce was among those quickly to extend the hand of friendship, at the same time expressing deep skepticism about education as a university discipline. Many of Royce's philosophical biases and psychological assumptions are now thought to be outmoded. Still, the reader may find that Royce shrewdly foresaw both the promises to be realized and the pitfalls to be encountered by those who sought to apply the insights of university research to the art of teaching.

This particular essay was written at the request of Nicholas Murray Butler, just after he had launched the Educational Review. *Like several other journals originating in this era, the* Review *was illustrative of the growing interest of university scholars in pedagogical studies and of the increasing effort to bring these scholars together with both the practitioners in the public schools and the normal-school teachers who trained them. Many articles by people from the latter groups accompanied the Royce essay; from the university side, Royce was joined by such men as Daniel Coit Gilman, Simon Patten, John Dewey, Joseph Jastrow, J. Mark Baldwin,*

* *Educational Review*, I (January, February, 1891), 15–25, 121–132.

John Bascom, and Albert Bushnell Hart, all of whom were, or were shortly to become, distinguished university professors.

The widely held assumption that academic professors of this period were either uninterested in, or actively hostile to, the study of pedagogy may be accurate with respect to the greater number of them. But the conclusion that the professors of education heard no friendly voice from influential colleagues in other departments is clearly false. Perhaps Royce's sympathetic "wait and see" attitude was more representative than is commonly thought. More careful institution-by-institution research may reveal that in many cases, the professors of education started out with considerable support but later alienated their defenders. Lawrence A. Cremin has argued plausibly, in The Transformation of the School, *that the educational reformers alienated, or allowed themselves to become isolated from, their intellectual supporters in the larger community. Possibly the same phenomenon occurred in microcosm on individual campuses.*

This opening number of a new review for the study of educational problems must naturally contain some article of a very general character, wherein the prospects and difficulties of the whole undertaking are discussed. That the editor should have intrusted to me the task of writing such a general survey of problems is not only an act of very kindly courtesy toward myself, but a sign of his own willingness to make the difficulties of the doctrine of education manifest from the outset. For the academic student of philosophy and of human nature loves the problems of his profession too much to regard or to depict them as easy; the university teacher is in general trained to reflect even more than to advise; and, for my own part, I have always felt unwilling to apply so pretentious and comforting a name as "Science" to any exposition of the laborious and problematic art of the educator. Yet if in this article I make doubts and difficulties prominent, as it is my office to do, I hope that before I am done it will be clear that my aim is as positive as my method is at times negative. A fragmentary, but still not wholly unsuggestive, program of investigations, such as may profitably be pursued by students of the art of education, an indication of certain significant needs of modern pedagogy, a warning against overhasty generalization, and still an encouragement to every loving observer of children to study the science of psychology without neglecting the intricacies of daily life, and to use wisely his own warm experience, rather than to trust to the mere letter of pedagogical dogmas—such are some of the things that I should like to furnish in my article. I have to make a number of critical and negative observations. I do not want to dishearten, rather do I long to strengthen the interest of teachers in the theoretical aspects of their profession.

I

A natural text for an essay upon the question of our title is just at present furnished by a widely known and much-discussed paper, read before the Academy of Sciences at Berlin, in July, 1888, and published in the proceedings of that body.[1] The author, Wilhelm Dilthey, Professor of Philosophy in the University of Berlin, is known as a many-sided and cautious student, especially of the more

[1] W. Dilthey, *Ueber die Möglichkeit einer allgemeingültigen pädagogischen Wissenschaft*, Sitzungsberichte der Berliner Akademie der Wissenschaften, 1888, pp. 807–832.

historical and humane aspects of philosophy. His excursion into the field of pedagogy is marked by all his usual caution and learning. His question is essentially our present one: "The Possibility of an universally valid Pedagogical Science." His beginning is negative and critical in tone; his statement of the limitations of the "universally valid doctrine of pedagogy" is highly noteworthy; his skepticism is keen; and yet the outcome of his whole article is, after all, hopeful, and even inspiring. I cannot do better than to begin by summarizing his views. I wish that I could hope to supplement them by anything that approached their knowledge of the subject, and their constructive power.

Dilthey begins by observing that all the prominent pedagogical systems, such as those of Herbart, Schleiermacher, Spencer, Bain, Beneke, Waitz, agree in one respect, that they pretend "to define the end of education, the value of the various branches of study, and the methods of instruction, in an universally valid fashion, and consequently for wholly different times and peoples." And this pretense, says Dilthey, at the very outset of his argument,—this pretense is precisely parallel to that of the old-fashioned theories of the state,—theories which, disregarding history and the varieties of circumstance, undertook to fix for all humanity the absolute forms of political life; and, in consequence, drove men to a revolt against the whole historical social order. This sort of theorizing belonged to the seventeenth and eighteenth centuries, culminated in the French Revolution, and has been replaced in our day by the historical method in political science,—a method which ignores the theoretical "Constitutions" of the *doctrinaires,* and which knows that political organizations are far too vital in their individual traits to be subject to any abstract formulation of the details of the "universally valid" social order. Now pedagogy, as embodied in such "systems" as have just been mentioned, represents precisely this old fashion of theorizing. Pedagogy arose in the seventeenth century, developed farther in the eighteenth, with the "naturalistic" theories, assumed a "natural" universality of aim and method as present, under all human conditions, for the educator, and so became the "comrade of natural theology, of the philosophy of law, and of abstract political economy." "Elsewhere," continues Dilthey, "the historical school has replaced naturalism"; pedagogy alone has, in this respect, refused to progress. As a fact, however, human nature cannot be adequately described through any abstractly universal formulation of its traits. Human nature, as a product of evolution, differs from nation to nation, from century to century. Nor is even an abstractly universal formulation of the ethical end of life a useful undertaking. "No moral system has ever yet been able to win universal recognition" (p. 808). The ends of life can only be defined with constant reference to the vital and growing motives and impulses of concrete humanity; and as the latter change so do the ends themselves, with the ethical systems that embody them. Hence the educator cannot hope to have defined for him, with abstract universality, either the material upon which he must always work,—namely, human nature,—nor the end toward which he must always aim,—namely, the highest moral perfection of his pupil. Both these matters are modified for him by the course of evolution, and by the actual social environment.

And yet, with all this necessary limitation, does there not remain a field for pedagogical science? Yes, answers Dilthey, in case, not the abstract description of human nature, and of the ends of living, but the truly psychological study of the typical forms of human evolution is pursued in the fashion which the historical and biological investigations of modern times have rendered possible. There are a few general laws that hold, not so much as to the content of human nature, but as to the fashion of its organic growth. These biological laws will turn out to have a practical significance. Human nature, namely, no matter how much it varies, in content or in ideals, is always in the first place a collection of impulses, of instincts, of feelings, and of tendencies *(Gefühle und Triebe)* which, from the outset of life, have a teleological character; that is, a character whereby they are adapted to the preservation of the individual in the environment in which the child is placed. These various reactions of feeling and impulse, however, these natural and teleological "reflexes," of each organism (such, for instance, as the reactions of hunger and of shyness, of curiosity and of friendliness), are at the outset, in the individual child, "not in organic connection with one another." No child begins with organized conduct. Its early impulses are as chaotic in their entirety as they are useful in their individual quality. "Observe the child; his desire for food, his avoidance of bodily injury, his social friendliness, appear all of them as isolated impulses, with no relation to the needs of his life as a whole, with no sense of their relative value. Like sunlight and shadow, one feeling chases another across his countenance" (p. 816). It is thus also with the savage. Usefulness of the single reaction, unteleological disorganization of the entirety of the reactions—such is the law of the early stages of human life. The growth, now, of mental life, "produces by continual adaptation those relations amongst" these elementary impulses, "whereby a teleological and complete unity of the character in the individual and in society" shall ideally come to pass. Such complete unity, to be sure, we none of us ever reach. No culture wins to the service of the organism and of the society the united and final co-operation of all human impulses. We all have our chaotic moments, and our anarchical desires. Nor has any form of civilization attained in its completeness the end of an entire organization of all the original impulses in full and mutual adaptation. Not yet, again, is an abstractly universal description of just what this unity of human life would be, accessible for us. And yet, thus, after all, is the general problem of education (not, to be sure, its general solution) to be defined for our "science." Not the one common end of life, in its precise content, but the type of human growth, in so far as it is growth, is after this fashion expressed. At the outset of life the human being is a chaos of impulses, each useful in itself, but all relatively independent. From the point of view of the highest ideal of growth, these impulses are to be brought from chaos to such complete order that not only in the individual, but in his relations to society, there shall be no chaos left, and only complete unity of life. And the educator is to do what he can to further such a growth in the child. Could we now describe in definite and material terms the content of this ideal of the perfect unity of character, could we tell what the man, and what the social order, would be like, in which the ideal were thus absolutely realized, then indeed we should have that "universal" theory of society and of education which the eighteenth century dreamed of. As a fact, however, we cannot describe the perfectly organized character because we have never seen it, and are subject in our judgment of what tends toward it to the vicissitudes and the accidents of our age and our nation. Any concrete account and picture of the ideal state that we may attempt will, therefore, have elements of chaos left in it. Any complete plan of education that we may devise will, furthermore, have defects, and only a transient significance. But there remains a sense in which the undertakings of pedagogy will be capable of scientific and general discussion. To the educator we in effect say: "Work against the chaos of impulses, by using the very impulses themselves as the material for good order. In a word, organize." Meanwhile, although the actual content of any attempted organization of life will be "historically determined," and so imperfect and transient, relatively general accounts can be given of processes that *do* increase the orderliness of the life of the child. Such accounts will take the form of "pedagogical rules," whose number Dilthey, of course, leaves indefinite. In short, scientific pedagogy, far from telling the teacher finally and completely just what human nature is, and must be, and just what to do with it, will be limited to pointing out what does, on the whole, tend toward good order and toward the organization of impulses into character. "This is the whole province of pedagogy," as a general science. Its application to the conditions of a particular time, nation, family, and child, will be a matter of art, not of science. And "therefore, no concrete educational questions can be solved in terms of an universally valid science." Such questions will always contain elements of uncertainty, will always require the practical skill of the individual educator, and will always receive answers that will vary with time and occasion.

The concluding section of Dilthey's paper is devoted to the mapping out of the province of pedagogy as thus defined. After an historical study of the growth of education, of its social relations, and of the general ways in which the child may be considered as at all plastic to the educator's purposes, scientific pedagogy would study the typical growth of the orderly life of impulse as it is manifested (1) in the games of childhood (universally human devices these for organizing infantile impulses), (2) in the consciously intellectual growth, that is, in the perceptive, attentive, memorizing, and reflective life of childhood and youth, and (3) in the parallel processes of the organization of the will. Rules would here be suggested by the science at every point; yet they would never be rules that the educator could immediately apply, except with constant reference to the conditions of his own nation, age, and child. Universal these rules would be, yet never universal in so far as they were precise guides in the concrete case. Aids they would be, but never substitutes for personal insight. In short, pedagogy, as a "science," would be a good staff and a bad crutch.

II

So far, in substance, Dilthey. As I summarize his discussion, I feel the necessary but disagreeable abstractness of my own form of statement. Brevity such as this must needs do injustice to so finely conceived and thoughtfully elaborated a paper as Dilthey's. In one sense, indeed, Dilthey's essay may be said to contain little novelty. To the philosophical student its conclusions will be in some measure familiar. It is in their application to our present problem that these words are so wholesome. The lesson of the historical as well as of the biological sciences is that when you undertake to discuss the growth of a complex organism you must not expect to deduce all the wealth of the details of this life from your account of the general type of the growth itself. The practical application of this lesson is not far to seek; and yet immature theorizers so often miss this application. Are you to interfere for a purpose with the growing organism, your knowledge of the type will be able to help you, and in so far there will be a possible science to guide your interference. If, then, you are an educator, and have to influence for a moral and social purpose the growth of a child, or of a youth, your knowledge, say of psychology, ought to aid you in your work; and in so far there will be a scientific element in education. Only there is all the while, the other, the more immediately practical side of your undertaking, namely, just the application of your insight into that typical growth as such, to the direction of your dealing with the individual living organism itself with the child, or with the youth. And just here it is the detail that will often concern you more than the type. Just what science abstracts from and ignores, just that you now most need to know. Your own surroundings, say as Frenchman or as American; your position as teacher of the sensitive child that needs tenderness, or of the rugged and sluggish child that needs awakening; your place as defender of this or of that worthy ideal, say of this religious creed, or of that, of this social tradition or of some other; your relation as private tutor to the individual child, or as public teacher to the larger class of many children; your experience of the accidental variations of just your own pupils' lives and destinies—all these things will properly interfere with anything like a truly scientific application of your pedagogical principles. You will degrade science,—not help your children,—if you persist in seeing only the "scientific" aspects of your pedagogy. True pedagogy is an art. A noteworthy German text-book of psychiatry, now on my library shelves, observes that the alienist's art, the care and cure of insanity, is one that "can indeed be learned, but that cannot be taught." And yet this text-book is itself a fine little compendium of the principles of the scientific treatment of the insane. Well, if alienism can be learned but not taught, how much more shall this not be the case with pedagogy! Disease seems indeed endlessly wealthy; nervous patients furnish to the alienist a world of capricious problems. But, nevertheless, the riches of health are greater still than the riches of disease; and the art of the true pedagogue could still less be taught in its entirety than can the art of the alienist. It is abstraction that simplifies; and abstraction is invaluable to science. But he who returns from science to life is a poor pupil if he has not learned the art of forgetting his formulas at the right moment, and of loving the live thing more than the describable type.

All these observations of mine are so far mere commonplaces. I almost repent having written them down. And yet, from one point of view, how necessary they seem to be—necessary, alas! not only for the pedants who are continually pretending to have discovered this or that complete and scientific and final "system of pedagogy," whereby alone all children may be saved,—but also for those unreflective lovers of child life who are indeed often so much better than the pedants, but who falsely imagine that because science cannot furnish a final "system" for all times, teachers, nations, and pupils, science is therefore worthless for the pedagogue. Both parties in such a controversy as that between these pedants and their unlearned opponents are in the wrong. There is no "science of education" that will not need constant and vast adaptation to the needs of this teacher or of that, constant modification in the presence of the live pupil, constant supplementing by the divine skill of the born teacher's instincts. This being true, there is, indeed, no "science of education" whose formulas will not need at the right moment to be forgotten. Yet, on the other hand, it makes great difference to you whether or no you do possess the science that you can be wise enough at the right moment to forget. Ignorance is one thing; the power voluntarily to ignore is quite another thing. The former is a weakness; the latter a high spiritual power. Universally valid your "system" never can be; therefore hold it not as system. But universally significant your scientific insight may become to you, if you once possess it, and can bear in mind that it is after all abstract, and yet noteworthy as an abstraction. Teachers then do need a scientific training for their calling. Instinct, unchastened by science, is blindly self-confident, and when it goes astray its fall from grace is irreparable; its very innocence then proves its doom. Teachers who know nothing of the reflective aspects of their calling, who do not try to comprehend as well as to love their pupils, who despise science because it cannot take the place of devotion and of instinct, may indeed be successful, and in any case, as I just said, their state, so long as by chance they do not go far astray, is vastly better than the present state of those pedants who have heard of modern science, of nerve-cells, and of apperception, and who forthwith have developed or copied some hundreds of systematic principles of "pedagogical method." The unreflective, I say, if the kindly light of nature leads them amid the encircling gloom of educational problems, are, indeed, so far, better than the pedants, who still think that God means to save his people by numbered or unnumbered paragraphs. But then, the pedants, after all, have been trying to learn, after their own fashion. They have formed a habit of learning. And if they are not already too old with their "science," they may perchance yet learn a little more, namely, that this, too, is vanity unless life supplements it. And whenever the pedants do learn this latter fact, they may take counsel of instinct and then become truly wise. For true wisdom is just reason set aglow by instinct. But the unlearned, on the other hand, are trusting only to the kindly light of nature itself. Therefore, if by chance some will-o'-the-wisp lead them astray, they will soon be finally unable to distinguish true from false, and will perish miserably. Healthy instinct outdoes vainly abstract learning. But imperfect learning can be corrected by more instruction; while untutored instinct, once corrupted, is lost.

To both parties to the controversy, then, to the pedants with their systems and to the unlearned with their instincts, we must offer the same suggestion as to the place of science in education. On the whole, special points of difference aside, I should agree with Dilthey. There is no universally valid science of pedagogy that is capable of any complete formulation, and of direct application to individual pupils and teachers. Nor will there ever be one so long as human nature develops, through crossbreeding in each new generation, individual types that never were there before; so long as history furnishes, in every age, novel social environments, new forms of faith, new ideals, a new industrial organization, and thus new problems for the educator. So long as these things go on, the educator's calling will be an art to whose beauty and complexity no science will be adequate. But, on the other hand, it is in vain that the inadequacy of science is made a sufficient excuse for knowing nothing of it. The more inadequate science is when alone, the more need of using it as a beginning when we set about our task. For the inadequacy of beginnings is always an indication that if we are to go further we ought at least to comprehend these beginnings themselves. Instinct needs science, not as a substitute, but as a partial support. Or, as I said, when you teach, you must know when to forget formulas; but you must have learned them in order to be able to forget them.

Yet enough of these generalities. It remains, in this paper, to point out certain portions of modern scientific research that promise to be most useful to the educator, within the limits that have been set in the foregoing to all such usefulness. Of pedagogy as a single and determinate science, I have always had serious suspicions; and the reasons for these I have now sufficiently formulated. That the teacher needs to know all that he can (1) of the subjects that he is to teach, and (2) of certain branches of science that promise to be of service to all teachers in general, whatever their special callings, I have never doubted. I reject the pedagogical system. I believe in the training of teachers. And this training, in so far as theoretical science can be of general service to its ends, I conceive to be determined by two considerations. The first is that the teacher should be, as I may word it, a naturalist, loving and, as far as may be, scientifically comprehending the life of childhood and youth, just as other naturalists try to comprehend the life of other organisms. The second is that the teacher should be a man of rational ideals, knowing what moral and social ends he wants to serve, and why he regards them as worthy. The second consideration, being, with all its importance, the one capable of the briefer treatment here, I shall put next in order. The first consideration will then be summarily dealt with as I close.

III

The teacher ought to be a man of ideals. The end of education is ethical. We desire to give the state a loyal subject, and society a worthy fellow-worker. To this end we labor with our pupil. Is it possible, then, to define in any scientific terms the moral ideal? Is it useful for the teacher to have studied ethics? To this question Dilthey has already responded, in his skeptical fashion, that, doubtless for good reason, "no moral system has yet won universal assent." Upon this side of pedagogy he lays small stress. The universal type of organization seems to be formulated by him in biological rather than in ethical terms. The child is to be made an harmonious living organism. The ends of life in the abstract cannot be universally defined. There are some who would regard Dilthey's skepticism in this matter with a mingling of dread and contempt. But to begin a discussion of the matter here would lead us too far afield in philosophy. I myself hold to the possibility of an universal ethical principle. But of matters strictly philosophical, this is no place to speak.

Yet all the while I feel the great difficulty of giving much practical aid to teachers, especially in this country, and at the present time, by demanding of even the more learned class of them an universal attention to theoretical ethics. The call to become conscious of one's moral ideals, both for the sake of one's own salvation, and for the sake of teaching others, is a call that comes to men in very different degrees and forms. Most commonly men feel the call in religious form, and for reasons closely connected with their faith. Our clergymen are our principal ethical advisers in this country; and, on the whole, it is well that this should be the case. Yet the religious is not the scientific spirit, although there is indeed no proper hostility between the passion to be holy, and the disposition to scrutinize scientifically what holiness is. I should be glad indeed if more of our teachers were early possessed of a share of the latter interest. We should have less philistinism in our schools, less hoodwinking of the childish conscience, less cowardice, less prudery, and more purity. But when I begin to ask who shall teach the teachers ethics, or how a critical and yet a truly reverent study of the great ideals and passions of humanity shall be popularized among them, I confess that I often see how philistinism is indeed far better than moral indifference, and how we might easily exchange the unwisdom of a portion of our customary clerical teaching of morality in this country for a kind of superficial reflection upon ethics, whose outcome would be very evil not only for our teachers, but for their pupils. As a dear friend of mine loves to say: Better strenuousness of devotion even to a false moral ideal, than a well-defined ideal but no strenuousness. In short, it is in the world of devotion to ideals that loyal instinct is most often the securer guide as against science.

Yet, despite all this, I am impelled to insist that the pedagogy of the future will have, as one of its duties, the encouragement of a reasonable ethical reflection among our teachers. I care indeed little, whether or not this reflection is generally pursued under a constant theological supervision. Theology is but the eternal religious passion of humanity, limited (and sometimes, indeed, even enchained) by the historical forces that have formed our relative and often transient imaginings about the world beyond sense. I believe in the passion, and in its true and eternal objects, too deeply not to love even its more transient forms. I do not find its ministers all equally wise guides as to ethical matters; and no wonder—since they do not find one another so. But they have done so much for us in this country that we can safely trust them in the future also to awaken higher reflective thought concerning ethical matters whenever the time clearly calls upon them to lead in this direction. And if ever an age showed signs that such a time was soon coming, surely the present age does so. I desire, then, to see more efforts, both within and without the churches, to train young teachers to a clear consciousness about duty and about its meaning. And I desire the study of ethics, without ceasing to be truly devout, to become also, as time goes on, more and more scientific in spirit and in content. Of the difficulties in the way of such a study in this country, in so far as they immediately concern the educator's business, the present widespread controversy concerning secular and religious instruction in the public schools gives a sufficient hint. In short, it is here the very value of ethical insight itself, both for the teacher and for his pupils, that renders a truly scientific treatment of moral questions, and a truly scientific training of teachers, especially difficult.

IV

The teacher, I say, should furthermore be a naturalist, and the department of natural history which directly concerns him is called psychology. The great successes of this infant science of late years have been indeed, of themselves, not without certain drawbacks for the practical teacher. Psychology is constantly growing as a whole more complex, and therefore more difficult to survey in its entirety; while, on the other hand, there have been recently developed within its field several very attractive, very special, and therefore very limited lines of research, which have drawn the public attention to themselves in such a fashion as to endanger, through hasty and one-sided generalizations, the proper sense of the magnitude and the difficulty of the whole science. In two directions, therefore, teachers who have looked to psychology for light as to the "science of education," have found their vision confused. Did they undertake to study psychology as one doctrine, they soon found themselves unable to grasp its manifold aspects. It confused them with the multiplicity of its researches. They were fain to go back to some older textbook, wherein, as in Spencer's *Psychology* all the "principles," as they used to be, were "unified." Hence the antiquated character of most of the compendious treatises on "pedagogical psychology." These may or may not be useful. Nearly all of them are very highly inadequate. But did the teacher, on the contrary, study his psychology only in monographs, then, of late years, certain attractive topics, such as hypnotism, for example, made themselves too prominent from among the mass of researches, and psychology seemed a wonderland of singular and one-sided generalizations. I have not yet seen a "system," or a "science of pedagogy," founded solely or mainly on the principle that the teacher ought to be primarily a hypnotizer; but I daily expect to find such a treatise announced. It would hardly be more one-sided or crude in its own way and day than Spencer's book on "Education" was in its time and environment. I doubt if it would have the same success; but it might succeed in bringing the "science" into a little fresh discredit. For the rest, to speak of more serious matters, I know of persons who have struggled with Preyer's admirable monograph on the *Mind of the Child,* in a vain endeavor to extract from its pages an infallible rule of procedure in dealing with very young children. The scientific monograph, even where it is of the best in itself, is in general dishearteningly limited as to its immediately practical outlook. Let me, then, in view of this difficulty, suggest what the direction is in which the study of psychology, as adapted to the use of teachers, ought to progress.

First, then, let the young teacher remember that it is not the "system" of a psychological science, not the exhaustive theory of the "powers of the human mind" that he needs, but rather the psychological spirit: that is, the love and the skill that are required for the purposes of mental diagnosis. When I said that the teacher should be a naturalist, I meant that he should be in the habit of observing the mental life of children for its own sake, and of judging the relative value of its moods and tendencies. For such observation of the live child his study of published psychological researches ought primarily to be meant to prepare him. Preyer's monograph on the *Mind of the Child* is, indeed, from one point of view, little more than a dry mass of details, with a few generalizations of a sort that no teacher will be able to use without much personal experience and skill. All this is necessary. It was not Preyer's first object to be pedagogical, but to contribute facts to his science. But see how useful just this collection of dry facts may become to the teacher if he reads the book, not for the pedagogical rules that he may have vainly hoped to find in it, but for the acquirement of the habit of observation that the book exemplifies. These early frowns and squintings of the infant, these cries that slowly become more vocal, and that prepare the way for language, these primitive gestures that form the basis for the later life of expression in the child —how vain to study them merely for the abstract pedagogical rules that somebody might try to deduce from them! But meanwhile, observe,—behind all this chaos of symptoms is the life, the consciousness, that is hereafter to grow so spiritual and significant. And this life, this consciousness, just that it is which you as teacher are to follow, to comprehend through sympathy if not through formulas, to diagnose; yes, to guide. Well then, get in the habit of examining, step by step with Preyer as he observes what mental processes there are going on here. When the infant learns to fix his gaze, when he studies his moving fist in the field of vision, when he bites his own foot as if to find whether it *is* his own, when he babbles his chaos of noises as a preparation for speech, follow the process, and follow it just as a training in mental diagnosis. You will not thus learn many formulas; but you will learn the art of comprehending mental symptoms. Just in this fashion naturalists always have to work. What is here in this live thing? Why does it move thus? What is it doing? What feelings does it appear to have? What type of rudimentary intelligence is it showing? Ask such things, not because they will give you a systematic theory, but because they will help you to form the habit of watching minds. For as teacher you will always be watching minds, yes, watching even more than judging them. And the habit of merely judging minds as good or evil, without observing what state it is, what mental coloring, what inner live process, that makes them good or evil; this habit, I say, is so ingrained in most of us that it is always hard to learn to substitute diagnosis for mere estimation, and a loving study of the process for mere external liking or disliking of the person. Yet just such study of the inner process is the larger part of a teacher's theoretical business. And that is why I counsel him to use his psychological reading rather to train his power of diagnosis, than to equip him with abstract pedagogical rules. The teacher who can make out what the child's actual state of mind is, has developed the true sort of psychological insight.

It is easy to illustrate how this attitude of the naturalist is worth training as part of a teacher's equipment. Lubbock, studying his bees and ants and wasps, to find just in what sense they had intelligence, learned no pedagogical principles. But his attitude was at least that of a relatively dispassionate diagnosis. In some fashion he learned to know the minds of his bees and ants, to look at their world as they must look at it. Well, a teacher in presence of a naughty child feels often as hopeless a sense of the remoteness and the mystery of this demoniac sullenness, obstinacy, cruelty, or disobedience, as ever an amateur naturalist may have felt as he looked at the marvelous doings of ants and of bees. We naturally take refuge from such mysteries by refusing to observe the mechanism of their symptoms, and by confining ourselves to mere external judgment. We dislike the naughty child and we tell him so. And up to a certain point this unsympathetic dislike of ours is indeed a useful discipline to the child. It stimulates his native social instincts to work against his morbid or hateful impulses. If he is strong enough to save himself, as he often is, our hatred and punishment set him at work to do so. But then this is but a small part of the humane task of the teacher. The child may not be strong enough to get out of the lonely mental dungeon of his naughtiness. In any case we must help him out if we can. He can't diagnose himself. He knows not whence comes the demon that torments him, or what power locks him in this prison. We must find out. That he is naughty we know, but what naughtiness is it? Is it, so to speak, cerebral naughtiness, or stomachic naughtiness? Are his bowels out of order, or is it his very strength of body that is here making his brain lustily wayward? So far the diagnosis is relatively a medical one. It becomes more strictly psychological when one has assured one's self that the mysterious cause is, on the whole, in the highest region; that it is "the boy" and not his stomach that is out of order, the brain cortex and not the alimentary canal that is primarily affected. Well, shall we here fall back on the merely external estimate and say, sternly, "So long as you choose to be wicked I can do nothing for you"? Sometimes, indeed, we have to be content with this. But the teacher wants, if possible, to do more. And here it is that he must become a psychologist, not in the systematic, but in the scrutinizing sense; not as scientific generalizer, but as observing naturalist, as collector of mental facts. What is going on in this mind? How does it feel to be naughty in just this way? Is it a case of the true "insistent impulse," or is it a chaos of angrily contending suggestions that come to the child from without? Is it "irritable weakness" of temperament, or is it confusion of head by reason of the manifoldness of the new impressions that are just now assailing the young brain? Or is it mere apathy, mental anæsthesia? Such questions may look technical. We don't ask them very often. When my own children are naughty, I am, alas! seldom in the mood to be psychological. But then, none the less, such questions ought to be asked, and intelligently, too, by the dispassionately scrutinizing teacher. They ought to be answered cautiously, after due time for observation. And the scrutinizing itself ought to be, so far as possible, as cool and as searching as Lubbock's study of the ants and bees or as Preyer's watching of the infantile eyes and fists. For only such examination will give insight, and only such insight will suggest the best means of cure.

As for the cure itself, pedagogical formulas will seldom prove sufficient for the case. If you could really get at the mechanism of naughtiness, you would probably see that as no two brains are alike, so no two children are ever naughty in precisely the same way. The diagnosis will, if acute and thorough, be pretty surely in part individual. But if you have understood the case, you will be nearer the cure; and your instincts and your experience will suggest that.

How rare, after all, is this love for mental diagnosis! How seldom do I meet with it! And yet, believe one who has tried the thing, that with all the obscurities and scientific dangers of the undertaking, there are few tasks more richly delightful than is the patient threading-out of the intricacies of a human mind, when once you can win its confidence and get at its secret. At the heart of its mystery there is always such a rich wealth of living ideas, interests, and passions! Its very naughtiness becomes for the careful observer a charming illustration of the many-sidedness of human nature, and for the humane observer a profound lesson as to how to help our fellow-men. You may love or you may hate the person in other relations, or you may even feel little interest one way or another in the ordinary and external aspects of his social life. But his inner soul is such a splendid world of mental symptoms and of living processes! Seldom do we get the chance thus to scrutinize our neighbor's heart. Only at certain times in childhood and in youth, at certain periods of mental weariness or weakness, the puzzled or frightened or suffering soul can thus willingly confide its heart's mystery to the humane observer. It is the teacher's privilege to find many such opportunities. I want him to study psychology in order that he may learn how to use them. And once having used them, he will find all his work strengthened and enlightened by them.

This first method in which theoretical psychology can be of service to the teacher having been disposed of, I can speak very briefly, and only by way of illustration, as

I close, of two sorts of inductions in modern psychology which seem to me to have especial pedagogical importance.

1. The growth of the intelligence is subject to certain still very imperfectly formulated laws, which, in a vague and general fashion began to be recognized in the last century, and which have been already much employed for pedagogical purposes. The higher processes of the intelligence are begun, and continually supported throughout our lives, by fitting sensory experiences. Upon a more or less accurate analysis of these, and of the perceptive processes that are dependent on them, has been founded the theory of object-teaching. Herbart's principle, since widely stated and applied, that involuntary attention not only precedes voluntary attention, but should always be employed by the teacher as a basis for the latter whenever that is possible, is another example of a pedagogical use of a psychological induction. This principle is embodied in that whole body of pedagogical doctrine about finding and appealing to a child's actual interest, which, in combination with the doctrine that sense-experience should always be used, when that is possible, as a basis for abstract thinking, and that perceptions must prepare the way for higher apperception, has done so much to revolutionize the practice of the modern teacher. The relation of attention and memory, of interest and retention, has again suggested to teachers a relatively scientific basis for much of their work. These are examples of the direct influence of psychology upon the theory of method. Their importance no one will deny. The imitation of the "science of teaching" in these directions is, however, quickly suggested by the story of the numberless pedagogical "fads" that, on the basis of a hasty assimilation of this or that psychological

induction concerning the processes of the intelligence, have lived or are living their day, doomed to an untimely death. Object-teaching, too, has had its absurdities; such recent "fads" again as the proclaiming of "manual training" as the one true way of salvation for our schools, will suggest what happens when the single induction pretends to take the place of the whole science, when the single device tries to crowd out nearly all the rest of the art, when one little idea that is most admirable in its place and time, like this very idea of "manual training," assumes a barbarous foreign name to give itself a loftier dignity, and presents itself as the one latest result of "science." Let us study the inductions of psychology; but let us finally anathematize the "fads," and all who trust in them. Science does not counsel individual, unchangeable, and infallible "methods." She corrects our errors; but she also shows that there is no royal road to the true method, which must vary with the particular educational problem that we have to solve. The devices of the pedagogue should take counsel of science; but they should be modest in their pretensions even after they have done so. Not every one who says "Psychology! Psychology!" shall be saved, nor is every deviser of a new fashion of appealing to the involuntary attention of childhood, or of strengthening its apperceptive processes, a prophet. Whenever we come to see that the possible devices of educational method are endlessly numerous, and that scientific psychology criticises but does not create them, while they themselves are the product of the practical experience and art of the educator, this part of our program for the training of teachers will be more wisely carried out than nowadays it often is. Study, then, the psychology of the intelligence, apply it as best you can to your methods of teaching, but beware of the "infallible methods." Such is my advice to teachers in this realm of their work.

2. A still more recent series of psychological inductions is suggested to us by what Dilthey has said of the typical growth of the human character from the chaotic state of the "primitive impulses" to the organized "teleological" unity of mature conduct. I need not dwell upon the general significance of the whole evolutionary point of view in modern psychology. I will venture, by way of illustration, to mention one aspect of it. I refer to the inductions as to the relations between the phenomena of mental growth and those of mental disease. Readers of Preyer will remember the analogies that he draws between the defects of childish speech, and the diseases of language in the adult. The phenomena of the will contain still more interesting analogies. The naughtiness of the child is indeed very often similar to what would constitute the symptoms of some form of criminal lunacy in the adult. The child shows you at times pathologically insistent impulses, as well as instances of pathological aboulia, or apathy of will, and many volitional derangements, too, of the explosive type, such as the violent outbursts of childish fury and malice in those who, when adults, will show little sign of burdens of this sort. The difference between the childish chaos of impulses and the derangements of mental disease, will usually lie in the fact that the childish defect, as such, is more frequently *merely* chaotic, so that you get what would be individual pathological symptoms in the adult, while you seldom get the whole context of any diseased type, unless, indeed, your child is actually diseased. But the analogy between childish defect and pathological symptoms is interesting; and science is making it constantly more so. I wish, therefore, that teachers who are looking for scientific

light as to the care of childhood, would take counsel, more frequently than they yet do, of the more enlightened expositors of modern mental pathology. Once more, the analogy in question must be used with caution, but the study of the nervous patient, who is, after all, in some fashion or other a child, cannot fail to suggest something to the cautious teacher. If it suggests nothing else, it will suggest to him just that humanity in mental diagnosis which the alienists learn to practice, and which unenlightened teachers so seldom possess. Study, then, the psychology of human evolution, and study it, too, in intimate connection with the psychology of mental defect and disease. Notice the analogy, and use the hints that the wise alienist gives as aids in your examination and training of children. Remember that the chaos of unreason in childhood is itself, in some measure, an incapacity of a relatively diseased sort, and that the wise teacher is a sort of physician who is to help the child toward getting that kind of health which we call maturity.

In the foregoing I have tried only to suggest, and, in the most inadequate fashion, to illustrate a very few of the relations between theoretical study and the teacher's business. To sum it all up in one word: Teaching is an art. Therefore there is indeed no science of education. But what there is, is the world of science furnishing material for the educator to study. If he seeks in that world for exact and universally valid direction, he will fail to get it, and deservedly fail, because science is not there to win anybody's bread, nor yet to furnish short and easy roads to even the noblest callings. But, on the other hand, if the teacher wants aid from the scientific spirit, and counsel from scientific inductions, there stands ready to his hand such assistance as, above all, psychology has to offer to the educator who desires to become a loving observer of the minds of children, and such assistance, too, as ethics may suggest to the man who is strong enough to grapple with deeper problems.

5. Albion W. Small:
"Demands of Sociology upon Pedagogy"*
(1896)

One of the more common elements in professional preservice curricula for teachers is the course in the "social foundations of education." The precise content of this course, to say nothing of the quality of instruction devoted to it, varies markedly from college to college. The social foundations courses have perhaps only two things in common: (1) they are, as Small suggests all social service instruction should be, interdisciplinary, and (2) they rest on the assumption that educators should "not rate themselves as leaders of children, but as makers of society," to use Small's phrase. Moreover, those who teach these courses have tended, for better or worse, to accept and extend Small's skepticism about the traditional packaging of instruction on the basis of the conventional disciplines. This point of view has affected not only the professional curriculum but also the curricula of the elementary school, the secondary school, and the colleges in which those who hold it have had a major influence.

Though the "social foundations of education" movement did not get its name or achieve widespread success until the 1930's, it was clearly foreshadowed in this essay.

* National Educational Association, *Addresses and Proceedings, 1896*, pp. 174–181, 184.

Albion W. Small

A colleague of John Dewey at the University of Chicago and one of those who helped establish sociology as a university discipline, Small had been a student of Lester Frank Ward, whose Dynamic Sociology *probably inspired the argument of this address. Among the later proponents of the social foundations movement were Dewey, himself indebted to Small, and students of both Dewey and Small.*

At the risk of seeming to reopen a closed incident of ancient history, this paper will take its departure from some passages in the report of the Committee of Ten. The present aim is to define a point of view quite different from that of the committee. In emphasizing the ends to be gained in education, rather than the means to be employed, the writer wishes to be understood as having in mind the whole school career. It is impossible within the limits of this paper to discuss laws or principles of variation which from this point of view should adapt methods to the learner's needs at different stages of mental growth.

"The principal end of all education," says the Conference on History, Civil Government, and Political Economy, "is training" (p. 168).

The sociologist develops this noncommittal response of the oracle into the following: The end of all education is, first, completion of the individual; second, implied in the first, adaptation of the individual to such co-operation with the society in which his lot is cast that he works at his best with the society in perfecting its own type, and consequently in creating conditions favorable to the development of a more perfect type of individual.

The Committee of Ten seems to have stopped at conclusions which tacitly assume that psychical processes in the individual are ends unto themselves. To be sure there are signs of a vague looking for of judgment from the tribunal of larger life upon the products of this pedagogy; but the standards of a real test seem to have had little effect upon the committee's point of view. We are told (p. 168) that the mind is chiefly developed in three ways: (a) by cultivating the powers of discriminating observation; (b) by strengthening the logical faculty . . . (c) by improving the processes of comparison, *i. e.*, the judgment. We are further told that "studies in language and the natural sciences are best adapted to cultivate the habits of observation; mathematics, for the training of the reasoning faculties; history and allied branches, to promote the mental power which we call the judgment." The naïvely mediæval psychology behind all this would be humorous if it were not tragical. I need not label the pedagogic philosophy with which my sociology allies itself when I declare that sociology, in common with the most intelligent pedagogy of today, refuses to classify educational material along these lines. In the first place education is not an affair of perception, reflection, and judgment alone. Education connotes the evolution of the whole personality, not merely of intelligence. In the second place, if I am not mistaken, a consensus is rapidly forming, both in pedagogy and in sociology, to the effect that action in contact with reality, not artificial selection of abstracted phases of reality, is the normal condition of maximum rate and symmetrical form of personal development. Sociology consequently joins with pedagogy in the aim to bring persons, whether in school or out of school, into as direct contact as possible with the concrete conditions in which all the functions of personality must be applied and controlled. In these conditions alone is that balanced action possible which is the desideratum alike of pedagogical and of social culture.

Once more the Committee of Ten was content to remain in the dismal shadows of the immemorial misconception that *disjecta membra* of representative knowledge are the sole available resource for educational development. I do not find among the fundamental concepts of the report any distinct recognition of the coherence of the things with which intelligent pedagogy aims to procure personal adaptation. The report presents a classified catalogue of subjects good for study, but there is no apparent conception of the cosmos of which these subjects are abstracted phases and elements. Nowhere in the report do I find recognition that education, when it is finished, is conscious conformity of individuals to the coherent cosmic reality of which they are parts. Until our pedagogy rests upon a more intelligent cosmic philosophy, and especially upon a more complete synthesis of social philosophy, we can hardly expect curricula to correspond with the essential conditions to which human action must learn to conform. A graduate of a leading eastern university, who is now making an impression upon American pedagogy, said recently that when he took his diploma, about ten years ago, history to his mind was a collection of material which he had studied under Professor A.; political economy another independent body of information which he studied under Professor B.; psychology, another isolated subject which he had studied under Professor C.; and so on through the curriculum. Not until six or seven years after graduation did it dawn upon him that each of these details of representation is an aspect of one reality which the pedagogy of the college had concealed in making the fragments prominent. The most serious consideration about this pedagogical perversion is not that it limits knowledge alone. It distorts the whole attitude of men towards the world. Instead of introducing men to reality it tricks them into belief that an unorganized procession of pedantic abstractions is reality.

The report of the Committee of Ten presents to the sociologist, therefore, this anomaly: It is a whole made up of parts, every one of which may possibly be accepted by sociology; but the totality, as presented by the committee, sociology must peremptorily reject. It is hot on the trail of pedagogical and sociological truth, without actually coming within sight of the truth. Human personality is not doomed to struggle forever *seriatim* with a long list of detached groups of facts in order to get its psychic and social development. The world of experience is one, not many. Pedagogy and sociology are discovering this unity by different processes, and as a consequence of their perception that educational material is essentially one, not many, pedagogy and sociology are bound to combine their demands for a complete change of front in education. The proper educator is reality, not conventionalized abstractions from reality. Hence the demand of the new pedagogy, supported heartily by the new sociology, that schooling, particularly in its earlier stages, shall be changed from an afflictive imposition upon life to a rationally concentrated accomplishment of a portion of life itself. Hence the correlated demand of the new pedagogy, also seconded by the new sociology, that, so far as conscious effort is made by instructors to supplement the education of action by the education of cognition, the objects of contemplation shall be kept real by being viewed constantly as organic parts of the one reality. They must no longer be made unreal through analytic segregation which leaves them standing apart as independent realities.

Having thus by negation challenged some of the implicit concessions of the Committee of Ten to the old dogmatic pedagogy, and to presociological concepts of reality, I pass to a positive definition of the outlook of sociology. I believe it to be also in the line of the pedagogy that will prevail.

Human experience is concerned with three knowable elements; First, man's material environment, inanimate, and animate; second, man himself as an individual, in all his characteristics, from his place in the animal kingdom, through his special physiology, psychology, and technology; third, man's associations or institutions. Sociology is the systematic attempt to reduce the reactions of these three elements—nature, man, institutions—to scientific form and expression. The inclusive reality which sociology finds comprehending both the processes and the products of these reactions is society, *i. e.*, individuals in association, within the conditions imposed by the material environment and modified by human achievement. The task set for each individual when he finds himself participant of this reality, is to accommodate himself to prevailing conditions in such a manner that he may both accomplish and enjoy a maximum share of the development which his stage in social evolution is empowered to accomplish.

This life task of men consequently sets the pedagogical task of teachers. The prime problem of education, as the sociologist views it, is how to promote adaptation of the individual to the conditions, natural and artificial, within which individuals live and move and have their being. It would not be in point to discuss here the relative place of action and cognition in progress toward this end. That belongs to pedagogical technology. I assume that both action and cognition are unchallenged means of modern pedagogy. With their proportions, and with the appropriate sequence at different stages of culture, sociology is not directly concerned. Sociology has no tolerance, however, for the pedantry that persists in carpentering together educational courses out of subjects which are supposed to exercise, first, the perceptive faculty, then the memory, then the language faculty, then the logical faculty, etc., etc., etc. On the contrary, every represented contact of a person with a portion of reality sooner or later calls into exercise every mental power of that person, probably in a more rational order and proportion than can be produced by an artificial process. Our business as teachers is primarily, therefore, not to train particular mental powers, but to select points of contact between learning minds and the reality that is to be learned. The mind's own autonomy will look out for the appropriate series of subjective mental processes. In the second place, our business as teachers is to bring these perceptive contacts of pupil's minds with points of objective reality into true association with all the remainder of objective reality, *i. e.,* we should help pupils, first, to see things, and second, to see things together as they actually exist in reality. In other words, the demand of sociology upon pedagogy is that it shall stop wet-nursing orphan mental faculties, and find out how to bring persons into touch with what objectively is, as it is. The mind itself will do the rest.

In pursuance of this demand, sociology necessarily becomes an active partisan upon one of the pedagogical doctrines over which educators are divided, viz.: sociology denies that the rational center for the concentration of studies is any science or group of sciences. The rational center is the student himself. Personal adaptation to life means the given person's organization of his contacts with reality. In other words, pedagogy should be the science of assisting youth to organize their contacts with reality; and by this I mean to organize these contacts with reality by both thought and action, and for both thought and action.

Relatively the world stands still during the school-age of any person. The pupil himself changes visibly almost every day. The reality with which the pupil can have conscious contact is defined therefore by the pupil's own powers and opportunities. At each stage, however, himself on the one hand, and nature, men, institutions, on the other hand, are the subject and object of adjustment. A changing self has the task of adaptation to a surrounding frame of things, which daily displays new mysteries and complexities. The teacher's task is to help the individual understand this environment, of which the pupil for a long time seems to himself to be the center. It is the teacher's business to help the pupil understand this whole environment as it is related to himself. Presently, if the pupil's perceptions grow more penetrating and comprehensive, his own personal interests cease to seem the pivot on which the world of experience turns. His personality becomes extended, and at the same time his egoism gets balanced with the personal equation of others whose interests appear. The child finds the complement of his egoism in the family, the school, the group of playmates, the community, and at last, if his education is complete, in society at large. Yet, at each varying diameter of comprehension, life, of which the child is at first to himself the center and circumference, and later life as a whole, of which to the last the individual is to himself in the final resort the most interesting part—life, either individual or social, is the ever-present reality which summarizes all that men can positively know. This central and inclusive reality varies, in representation, from socially unrelated individual life to a conception of individual life enlarged by evolved social consciousness into a function of the more abiding reality. This human career, either as pursued for himself by the socially unconscious individual, or as a mingling of the individual with others associated by force of circumstances in pursuing purposes which none perfectly comprehend,—this life of men alike in nature, within conditions, imposing common limitations upon nature,— is the whole of man's range of positive experience and scientific observation. Sociology consequently demands of educators that they shall elaborate available aids, first, to perception by the individual of the relation of part to part in this inclusive reality—the life of men in society; second, that educators shall perfect influences to promote adjustment of individuals to their appropriate functions within this whole. The part of the problem which I have at present in mind is the proper direction and organization of the pupil's perceptions. So far as the subject-matter of sociology is concerned, everything knowable and worth knowing is a fact or a relation helping to make up this complexity which we call society or social life. The important claim of sociology in this connection is that this reality, like poverty, we have always with us. This reality as a connected whole, related to the pupil, is always the natural and rational means of education. A sequence of studies, in the sense that the pupil is to be enjoined from intelligent contact with portions of reality until other portions have had their turn, is a monstrous perversion of the conditions of education. All reality, the whole plexus of social life, is continually confronting the pupil. No "subject" abstracted from this actual whole is veracious to the pupil unless he is permitted to see it as a part of the whole. It is a misconstruction of reality to think and accordingly to act as though one kind of knowledge belongs to one age and another to another. The whole vast mystery of life, in all its processes and conditions, confronts the child as really as it does the sage. It is the business of the educator to help the child interpret the part by the whole. Education from the beginning should be an initiation into science, language, philosophy, art, and political action in the largest sense. When we shall have adopted a thoroughly rational pedagogy, the child will begin to learn everything the moment he begins to learn anything.

Am I demanding a pedagogy which presupposes one philosopher as teacher and another as pupil? Certainly. Every teacher ought to be a philosopher. Every child already is one till conventionality spoils him. More than that, he is also scientist, poet, and artist in embryo, and would mature in all these characters if we did not stunt him with our bungling. I would revive Rousseau's cry, "Return to nature!" but in a sense of which Rousseau never dreamed,—not nature in the burlesque of our ignorant preconceptions, but nature scientifically explored, nature, the universal law of which is to own the sway of rational mind.

I am not asserting that grammar, and geometry, and geography, and geology, and history, and economics, and psychology, and ethics, as such, should be taught in the nursery. I am asserting that in the cradle the child begins to be in contact with that nature and society of which all these are phases and products, and reports. Sociology demands for the child, from the cradle to his second childhood, opportunities for such frank contact with life that its various aspects will confide to him their mystery in its real relations with the other elements of life. Sociology demands of the tutors and governors who lead the child through the formal part of education, that they shall pilot Wilhelm Meister so discreetly through his years of apprenticeship that he shall learn his world at the smallest expense and with least cause for regret both to others and to himself. Whether this citizen of the world shall ever learn to construe life in terms of the conventional sciences is an entirely secondary matter. The main thing is that, from the beginning, he shall learn to know himself and his world truly—so far as he knows at all,—in all essential relations. This involves the learning of such sciences as he does acquire in the character of excerpts from the whole book of knowledge, not as self-sufficient knowledges.

I repeat that sociology values subjects of study for reasons quite different from those traditionally alleged. Physical, biological, and social science, with the products of human thought deposited in literature, are worthy of study not because they are tonics for various kinds of mental impotence, but because they are, and only in so far as they are, revealers of man himself and of the life of which he is both creator and creature.

Without alluding further to other departments of knowledge, I may apply what I have said to the subject-matter of the social sciences in particular.

Sociology demands with equal confidence: first, that for everybody the study of *society* shall begin with the nursing bottle, and continue so long as social relations continue; second, that for most people the study of *sociology* shall never begin at all. If the argument thus far has provoked expectation that I shall recommend the introduction of sociology into the curriculum of the lower schools, as the needed corrective of educational defects, the inference is decidedly at fault. Only exceptional pupils should study sociology earlier than their senior year in college, and probably these few would do better to defer the study till after taking the bachelor's degree. While sociology proper is not a desirable subject for young pupils, our educational methods will be miserably inadequate to their social function till every teacher, from the kindergarten on, is sufficiently instructed in sociology to put all his teaching in the setting which the sociological view-point affords. This implies, of course, that the function of education must one day be taken so seriously that only men and women who have more than the bachelor's preparation will be entrusted with its direction.

The study of society which we may reasonably demand in our schools and colleges today must and should be chiefly in connection with the subjects physiography, political geography, anthropology, ethnology, history, civics, and economics. The sociological demand with reference to these subjects is that instruction in them shall be rationalized in the same way that the teaching of geography has been reformed during my recollection. . . .

Sociology demands of educators, finally, that they shall not rate themselves as leaders of children, but as makers of society. Sociology knows no means for the amelioration or reform of society more radical than those of which teachers hold the leverage. The teacher who realizes his social function will not be satisfied with passing children to the next grade. He will read his success only in the record of men and women who go from the school eager to explore wider and deeper these social relations, and zealous to do their part in making a better future. We are the dupes of faulty analysis if we imagine that schools can do much to promote social progress until they are motived by this insight and this temper.

6. John Dewey:
"The Relation of Theory to Practice in Education"*
(1904)

Not infrequently, the historian encounters a dusty copy of a near-forgotten essay of a seminal thinker and says to himself, "This is one of the best things he ever wrote. Why has it been neglected while other essays, treating less significant ideas less clearly, are widely cited?"

Such was my first reaction to the article here reproduced. One suspects, perhaps unkindly, that it has been neglected by some because it appeared in a volume whose title carries the words "education of teachers," and that they have assumed that a distinguished philosopher would not devote his most serious thought to such a pedestrian subject. Others may have been too busy reforming teacher education to expect that anything fruitful was said so long ago. But whatever the reasons, the neglect has been unfortunate. The essay not only contains provocative suggestions for teacher education; it also helps clarify Dewey's ideas about the relationship of subject matter—the conventional disciplines—to life and learning and about the relationship of theoretical insight to practical activity in general.

To be sure, the article is dated. It was written as the

* National Society for the Scientific Study of Education, *The Relation of Theory to Practice in the Education of Teachers*, Third Yearbook, Part I (Bloomington, Ill.: Public School Publishing Co., 1904), pp. 9–30.

Oswego-Pestalozzian fad was giving way to the newer Herbartian fancy, a time in which hope for a universal pedagogical method still ran strong. But it was also a time in which the problems of integrating subject-matter preparation with professional instruction and relating educational theory to student-teaching were relatively new. During this period, one could discuss these problems without encountering the rigidities of thought that now make it difficult to take a fresh look.

The essay has not been without influence. As has been the fate of many of Dewey's phrases, "professional laboratory activities" has become part of the liturgy in some circles. Those who insist that the phrase be used to designate experiences in which the prospective teacher is brought into direct contact with elementary- or secondary-school youngsters are suspicious, almost instinctively it seems, of those who describe student-teaching as "apprenticeship," a term Dewey contrasted with "professional laboratory activities." Early proponents of professional laboratory activities read this essay and were influenced by their understanding of it. But one encounters more recent advocates who seem to sense but vaguely how laboratory activity differs from apprenticeship; they assume simply that the former is good, the latter bad. Interestingly enough, those who argue that teachers should be prepared by a "liberal education followed by an extensive apprenticeship" in turn suspect —and again, it seems, almost instinctively—those who speak of professional laboratory activities. Here the value connotations are reversed. Thus, we have another case in which phrases Dewey placed in contrast to illuminate fundamental concerns have been stripped of the meanings he gave them and left to stand alone as battle flags.

This article will make it clear that he hoped to accomplish more.

It is difficult, if not impossible, to define the proper relationship of theory and practice without a preliminary discussion, respectively, (1) of the nature and aim of theory; (2) of practice.[1]

A. I shall assume without argument that adequate professional instruction of teachers is not exclusively theoretical, but involves a certain amount of practical work. The primary question as to the latter is the aim with which it shall be conducted. Two controlling purposes may be entertained so different from each other as radically to alter the amount, conditions, and method of practice work. On one hand, we may carry on the practical work with the object of giving teachers in training working command of the necessary tools of their profession; control of the technique of class instruction and management; skill and proficiency in the work of teaching. With this aim in view, practice work is, as far as it goes, of the nature of apprenticeship. On the other hand, we may propose to use practice work as an instrument in making real and vital theoretical instruction; the knowledge of subject-matter and of principles of education. This is the laboratory point of view.

The contrast between the two points of view is obvious; and the two aims together give the limiting terms within which all practice work falls. From one point of view, the aim is to form and equip the actual teacher;

[1] This paper is to be taken as representing the views of the writer, rather than those of any particular institution in an official way; for the writer thought it better to discuss certain principles that seem to him fundamental, rather than to define a system of procedure.

the aim is immediately as well as ultimately practical. From the other point of view, the *immediate* aim, the way of getting at the ultimate aim, is to supply the intellectual method and material of good workmanship, instead of making on the spot, as it were, an efficient workman. Practice work thus considered is administered primarily with reference to the intellectual reactions it incites, giving the student a better hold upon the educational significance of the subject-matter he is acquiring, and of the science, philosophy, and history of education. Of course, the *results* are not exclusive. It would be very strange if practice work in doing what the laboratory does for a student of physics or chemistry in way of securing a more vital understanding of its principles, should not at the same time insure some skill in the instruction and management of a class. It would also be peculiar if the process of acquiring such skill should not also incidentally serve to enlighten and enrich instruction in subject-matter and the theory of education. None the less, there is a fundamental difference in the conception and conduct of the practice work according as one idea or the other is dominant and the other subordinate. If the primary object of practice is acquiring skill in performing the duties of a teacher, then the amount of time given to practice work, the place at which it is introduced, the method of conducting it, of supervising, criticising, and correlating it, will differ widely from the method where the laboratory ideal prevails; and *vice versa.*

In discussing this matter, I shall try to present what I have termed the laboratory, as distinct from the apprentice idea. While I speak primarily from the standpoint of the college, I should not be frank if I did not say that I believe what I am going to say holds, *mutatis mutandis,* for the normal school as well.

I. I first adduce the example of other professional

schools. I doubt whether we, as educators, keep in mind with sufficient constancy the fact that the problem of training teachers is one species of a more generic affair—that of training for professions. Our problem is akin to that of training architects, engineers, doctors, lawyers, etc. Moreover, since (shameful and incredible as it seems) the vocation of teaching is practically the last to recognize the need of specific professional preparation, there is all the more reason for teachers to try to find what they may learn from the more extensive and matured experience of other callings. If now we turn to what has happened in the history of training for other professions, we find the following marked tendencies:

1. The demand for an increased amount of scholastic attainments as a prerequisite for entering upon professional work.

2. Development of certain lines of work in the applied sciences and arts, as centers of professional work; compare, for example, the place occupied by chemistry and physiology in medical training at present, with that occupied by chairs of "practice" and of *"materia medica"* a generation ago.

3. Arrangement of the practical and quasi-professional work upon the assumption that (limits of time, etc., being taken into account) the professional school does its best for its students when it gives them typical and intensive, rather than extensive and detailed, practice. It aims, in a word, at *control of the intellectual methods* required for personal and independent mastery of practical skill, rather than at turning out at once masters of the craft. This arrangement necessarily involves considerable postponement of skill in the routine and technique of the profession, until the student, after graduation, enters upon the pursuit of his calling.

John Dewey

These results are all the more important to us because other professional schools mostly started from the same position which training schools for teachers have occupied. Their history shows a period in which the idea was that students ought from the start to be made as proficient as possible in practical skill. In seeking for the motive forces which have caused professional schools to travel so steadily away from this position and toward the idea that practical work should be conducted for the sake of vitalizing and illuminating *intellectual* methods two reasons may be singled out:

a) First, the limited time at the disposal of the schools, and the consequent need of economy in its employ. It is not necessary to assume that apprenticeship is of itself a bad thing. On the contrary, it may be admitted to be a good thing; but the time which a student spends in the training school is short at the best. Since short, it is an urgent matter that it be put to its most effective use; and, relatively speaking, the wise employ of this short time is in laying scientific foundations. These cannot be adequately secured when one is doing the actual work of the profession, while professional life does afford time for acquiring and perfecting skill of the more technical sort.

b) In the second place, there is inability to furnish in the school adequate conditions for the best acquiring and using of skill. As compared with actual practice, the best that the school of law or medicine can do is to provide a somewhat remote and simulated copy of the real thing. For such schools to attempt to give the skill which comes to those adequately prepared, insensibly and unavoidably in actual work, is the same sort of thing as for grammar schools to spend months upon months in trying to convey (usually quite unsuccessfully) that skill in commercial arithmetic which comes, under penalty of practical failure, in a few weeks in the bank or counting-house.

It may be said that the analogy does not hold good for teachers' training schools, because such institutions have model or practice departments, supplying conditions which are identical with those which the teacher has to meet in the actual pursuit of his calling. But this is true at most only in such normal schools as are organized after the Oswego pattern—schools, that is to say, where the pupil-teacher is given for a considerable period of time the entire charge of instruction and discipline in the class-room, and does not come under a room critic-teacher. In all other cases, some of the most fundamentally significant features of the real school are reduced or eliminated. Most "practice schools" are a compromise. In theory they approximate ordinary conditions. As matter of fact, the "best interests of the children" are so safeguarded and supervised that the situation approaches learning to swim without going *too* near the water.

There are many ways that do not strike one at first glance, for removing the conditions of "practice work" from those of actual teaching. Deprivation of responsibility for the discipline of the room; the continued presence of an expert ready to suggest, to take matters into his own hands; close supervision; reduction of size of group taught; etc., etc., are some of these ways. The topic of "lesson plans" will be later referred to in connection with another topic. Here they may be alluded to as constituting one of the modes in which the conditions of the practice-teacher are made unreal. The student who prepares a number of more or less set lessons; who then has those lesson plans criticised; who then has his actual teaching criticised from the standpoint of success in carrying out the prearranged plans, is in a totally different

John Dewey

attitude from the teacher who has to build up and modify his teaching plans as he goes along from experience gained in contact with pupils.

It would be difficult to find two things more remote from each other than the development of subject-matter under such control as is supplied from actual teaching, taking effect through the teacher's own initiative and reflective criticism, and its development with an eye fixed upon the judgment, presumed and actual, of a superior supervisory officer. Those phases of the problem of practice teaching which relate more distinctly to responsibility for the discipline of the room, or of the class, have received considerable attention in the past; but the more delicate and far-reaching matter of intellectual responsibility is too frequently ignored. Here centers the problem of securing conditions which will make practice work a genuine apprenticeship.

II. To place the emphasis upon the securing of proficiency in teaching and discipline *puts the attention of the student-teacher in the wrong place, and tends to fix it in the wrong direction*—not wrong absolutely, but relatively as regards perspective of needs and opportunities. The would-be teacher has some time or other to face and solve two problems, each extensive and serious enough by itself to demand absorbing and undivided attention. These two problems are:

1. Mastery of subject-matter from the standpoint of its educational value and use; or, what is the same thing, the mastery of educational principles in their application to that subject-matter which is at once the material of instruction and the basis of discipline and control;

2. The mastery of the technique of class management.

This does not mean that the two problems are in any way isolated or independent. On the contrary, they are strictly correlative. *But the mind of a student cannot give equal attention to both at the same time.*

The difficulties which face a beginning teacher, who is set down for the first time before a class of from thirty to sixty children, in the responsibilities not only of instruction, but of maintaining the required order in the room as a whole, are most trying. It is almost impossible for an old teacher who has acquired the requisite skill of doing two or three distinct things simultaneously—skill to see the room as a whole while hearing one individual in one class recite, of keeping the program of the day and, yes, of the week and of the month in the fringe of consciousness while the work of the hour is in its center—it is almost impossible for such a teacher to realize all the difficulties that confront the average beginner.

There is a technique of teaching, just as there is a technique of piano-playing. The technique, if it is to be educationally effective, is dependent upon principles. But it is possible for a student to acquire outward form of method without capacity to put it to genuinely educative use. As every teacher knows, children have an inner and an outer attention. The inner attention is the giving of the mind without reserve or qualification to the subject in hand. It is the first-hand and personal play of mental powers. As such, it is a fundamental condition of mental growth. To be able to keep track of this mental play, to recognize the signs of its presence or absence, to know how it is initiated and maintained, how to test it by results attained, and to test *apparent* results by it, is the supreme mark and criterion of a teacher. It means insight into soul-action, ability to discriminate the genuine from the sham, and capacity to further one and discourage the other.

External attention, on the other hand, is that given to

the book or teacher as an independent object. It is manifested in certain conventional postures and physical attitudes rather than in the movement of thought. Children acquire great dexterity in exhibiting in conventional and expected ways the *form* of attention to school work, while reserving the inner play of their own thoughts, images, and emotions for subjects that are more important to them, but quite irrelevant.

Now, the teacher who is plunged prematurely into the pressing and practical problem of keeping order in the schoolroom has almost of necessity to make supreme the matter of external attention. The teacher has not yet had the training which affords psychological insight—which enables him to judge promptly (and therefore almost automatically) the kind and mode of subject-matter which the pupil needs at a given moment to keep his attention moving forward effectively and healthfully. He does know, however, that he must maintain order; that he must keep the attention of the pupils fixed upon his own questions, suggestions, instructions, and remarks, and upon their "lessons." The inherent tendency of the situation therefore is for him to acquire his technique in relation to the outward rather than the inner mode of attention.

III. Along with this fixation of attention upon the secondary at the expense of the primary problem, *there goes the formation of habits of work which have an empirical, rather than a scientific, sanction.* The student adjusts his actual methods of teaching, not to the principles which he is acquiring, but to what he sees succeed and fail in an empirical way from moment to moment: to what he sees other teachers doing who are more experienced and successful in keeping order than he is; and to the injunctions and directions given him by others. In this way the controlling habits of the teacher finally get fixed with comparatively little reference to principles in the psychology, logic, and history of education. In theory, these latter are dominant; in practice, the moving forces are the devices and methods which are picked up through blind experimentation; through examples which are not rationalized; through precepts which are more or less arbitrary and mechanical; through advice based upon the experience of others. Here we have the explanation, in considerable part at least, of the dualism, the unconscious duplicity, which is one of the chief evils of the teaching profession. There is an enthusiastic devotion to certain principles of lofty theory in the abstract —principles of self-activity, self-control, intellectual and moral—and there is a school practice taking little heed of the official pedagogic creed. Theory and practice do not grow together out of and into the teacher's personal experience.

Ultimately there are two bases upon which the habits of a teacher as a teacher may be built up. They may be formed under the inspiration and constant criticism of intelligence, applying the best that is available. This is possible only where the would-be teacher has become fairly saturated with his subject-matter, and with his psychological and ethical philosophy of education. Only when such things have become incorporated in mental habit, have become part of the working tendencies of observation, insight, and reflection, will these principles work automatically, unconsciously, and hence promptly and effectively. And this means that practical work should be pursued primarily with reference to its reaction upon the professional pupil in making him a thoughtful and alert student of education, rather than to help him get immediate proficiency.

For immediate skill may be got at the cost of power to go on growing. The teacher who leaves the professional school with power in managing a class of children may appear to superior advantage the first day, the first week, the first month, or even the first year, as compared with some other teacher who has a much more vital command of the psychology, logic, and ethics of development. But later "progress" may with such consist only in perfecting and refining skill already possessed. Such persons seem to know how to teach, but they are not students of teaching. Even though they go on studying books of pedagogy, reading teachers' journals, attending teachers' institutes, etc., yet the root of the matter is not in them, unless they continue to be students of subject-matter, and students of mind-activity. Unless a teacher is such a student, he may continue to improve in the mechanics of school management, but he can not grow as a teacher, an inspirer and director of soul-life. How often do candid instructors in training schools for teachers acknowledge disappointment in the later career of even their more promising candidates! They seem to strike twelve at the start. There is an unexpected and seemingly unaccountable failure to maintain steady growth. Is this in some part due to the undue premature stress laid in early practice work upon securing immediate capability in teaching?

I might go on to mention other evils which seem to me to be more or less the effect of this same cause. Among them are the lack of intellectual independence among teachers, their tendency to intellectual subserviency. The "model lesson" of the teachers' institute and of the educational journal is a monument, on the one hand, of the eagerness of those in authority to secure immediate practical results at any cost; and, upon the other, of the willingness of our teaching corps to accept without inquiry or criticism any method or device which seems to promise good results. Teachers, actual and intending, flock to those persons who give them clear-cut and definite instructions as to just how to teach this or that.

The tendency of educational development to proceed by reaction from one thing to another, to adopt for one year, or for a term of seven years, this or that new study or method of teaching, and then as abruptly to swing over to some new educational gospel, is a result which would be impossible if teachers were adequately moved by their own independent intelligence. The willingness of teachers, especially of those occupying administrative positions, to become submerged in the routine detail of their callings, to expend the bulk of their energy upon forms and rules and regulations, and reports and percentages, is another evidence of the absence of intellectual vitality. If teachers were possessed by the spirit of an abiding student of education, this spirit would find some way of breaking through the mesh and coil of circumstance and would find expression for itself.

B. Let us turn from the practical side to the theoretical. What must be the aim and spirit of theory in order that practice work may really serve the purpose of an educational laboratory? We are met here with the belief that instruction in theory is merely theoretical, abstruse, remote, and therefore relatively useless to the teacher as a teacher, unless the student is at once set upon the work of teaching; that only "practice" can give a motive to a professional learning, and supply material for educational courses. It is not infrequently claimed (or at least unconsciously assumed) that students will not have a professional stimulus for their work in subject-matter and in educational psychology and history, will not have any outlook upon their relation to education, unless

John Dewey

these things are immediately and simultaneously reinforced by setting the student upon the work of teaching. But is this the case? Or are there practical elements and bearings already contained in theoretical instruction of the proper sort?

I. Since it is impossible to cover in this paper all phases of the philosophy and science of education, I shall speak from the standpoint of psychology, believing that this may be taken as typical of the whole range of instruction in educational theory as such.

In the first place, beginning students have without any reference to immediate teaching a very large capital of an exceedingly practical sort in their own experience. The argument that theoretical instruction is merely abstract and in the air unless students are set at once to test and illustrate it by practice-teaching of their own, *overlooks the continuity of the class-room mental activity with that of other normal experience.* It ignores the tremendous importance for educational purposes of this continuity. Those who employ this argument seem to isolate the psychology of learning that goes on in the schoolroom from the psychology of learning found elsewhere.

This isolation is both unnecessary and harmful. It is unnecessary, tending to futility, because it throws away or makes light of the greatest asset in the student's possession—the greatest, moreover, that ever will be in his possession—his own direct and personal experience. There is every presumption (since the student is not an imbecile) that he has been learning all the days of his life, and that he is still learning from day to day. He must accordingly have in his own experience plenty of practical material by which to illustrate and vitalize theoretical principles and laws of mental growth in the process of learning. Moreover, since none of us is brought up under ideal conditions, each beginning student has plenty of practical experience by which to illustrate cases of arrested development—instances of failure and maladaptation and retrogression, or even degeneration. The material at hand is pathological as well as healthy. It serves to embody and illustrate both achievement and failure, in the problem of learning.

But it is more than a serious mistake (violating the principle of proceeding from the known to the unknown) to fail to take account of this body of practical experience. Such ignoring tends also to perpetuate some of the greatest evils of current school methods. Just because the student's attention is not brought to the point of recognizing that *his own* past and present growth is proceeding in accordance with the very laws that control growth in the school, and that there is no psychology of the schoolroom different from that of the nursery, the playground, the street, and the parlor, he comes unconsciously to assume that education in the class-room is a sort of unique thing, having its own laws.[2] Unconsciously, but none the less surely, the student comes to believe in certain "methods" of learning, and hence of teaching which are somehow especially appropriate to the school—which somehow have their particular residence and application there. Hence he comes to believe in the potency for schoolroom purposes of materials, methods, and devices which it never occurs to him to trust to in his experience outside of school.

I know a teacher of teachers who is accustomed to say that when she fails to make clear to a class of teachers

[2] There is where the plea for "adult" psychology has force. The person who does not know himself is not likely to know others. The adult psychology ought, however, to be just as genetic as that of childhood.

some point relative to children, she asks these teachers to stop thinking of their own pupils and to think of some nephew, niece, cousin, some child of whom they have acquaintance in the unformalities of home life. I do not suppose any great argument is needed to prove that breach of continuity between learning within and without the school is the great cause in education of wasted power and misdirected effort. I wish rather to take advantage of this assumption (which I think will be generally accepted) to emphasize the danger of bringing the would-be teacher into an abrupt and dislocated contact with the psychology of the schoolroom—abrupt and dislocated because not prepared for by prior practice in selecting and organizing the relevant principles and data contained within the experience best known to him, his own.[3]

From this basis, a transition to educational psychology may be made in observation of the teaching of others—visiting classes. I should wish to note here, however, the same principle that I have mentioned as regards practice work, specifically so termed. The first observation of instruction given by model- or critic-teachers should not be too definitely practical in aim. The student should not be observing to find out how the good teacher does it, in order to accumulate a store of methods by which he also may teach successfully. He should rather observe with reference to seeing the interaction of mind, to see how teacher and pupils react upon each other—how mind answers to mind. Observation should at first be conducted

[3] It may avoid misapprehension if I repeat the word *experience*. It is not a *metaphysical* introspection that I have in mind, but the process of turning back upon one's own experiences, and turning them over to see how they were developed, what helped and hindered, the stimuli and the inhibitions both within and without the organism.

from the psychological rather than from the "practical" standpoint. If the latter is emphasized before the student has an independent command of the former, the principle of imitation is almost sure to play an exaggerated part in the observer's future teaching, and hence at the expense of personal insight and initiative. What the student needs most at this stage of growth is ability to see what is going on in the minds of a group of persons who are in intellectual contact with one another. He needs to learn to observe psychologically—a very different thing from simply observing how a teacher gets "good results" in presenting any particular subject.

It should go without saying that the student who has acquired power in psychological observation and interpretation may finally go on to observe more technical aspects of instruction, namely, the various methods and instrumentalities used by a good teacher in giving instruction in any subject. If properly prepared for, this need not tend to produce copiers, followers of tradition and example. Such students will be able to translate the practical devices which are such an important part of the equipment of a good teacher over into their psychological equivalents; to know not merely as a matter of brute fact that they do work, but to know how and why they work. Thus he will be an independent judge and critic of their proper use and adaptation.

In the foregoing I have assumed that educational psychology is marked off from general psychology simply by the emphasis which it puts upon two factors. The first is the stress laid upon a certain end, namely, growth or development—with its counterparts, arrest and adaptation. The second is the importance attached to the social factor—to the mutual interaction of different minds with each other. It is, I think, strictly true that no educational procedure nor pedagogical maxim can be derived directly from pure psychological data. The psychological data taken without qualification (which is what I mean by their being pure) cover everything and anything that may take place in a mind. Mental arrest and decay occur according to psychological laws, just as surely as do development and progress.

We do not make practical maxims out of physics by telling persons to move according to laws of gravitation. If people move at all, they *must* move in accordance with the conditions stated by this law. Similarly, if mental operations take place at all, they *must* take place in accordance with the principles stated in correct psychological generalizations. It is superfluous and meaningless to attempt to turn these psychological principles directly into rules of teaching. But the person who knows the laws of mechanics knows the conditions of which he must take account when he wishes to reach a certain end. He knows that *if* he aims to build a bridge, he must build it in a certain way and of certain materials, or else he will not have a bridge, but a heap of rubbish. So in psychology. Given an end, say promotion of healthy growth, psychological observations and reflection put us in control of the conditions concerned in that growth. We know that if we are to get that *end,* we must do it in a certain way. It is the subordination of the psychological material to the problem of effecting growth and avoiding arrest and waste which constitutes a distinguishing mark of educational psychology.

I have spoken of the importance of the social factor as the other mark. I do not mean, of course, that general theoretical psychology ignores the existence and significance of the reaction of mind to mind—though it would be within bounds to say that till recently the social side was an unwritten chapter of psychology. I mean that considerations of the ways in which one mind responds to the stimuli which another mind is consciously or unconsciously furnishing possess a relative importance for the educator which they have not for the psychologist as such. From the teacher's standpoint, it is not too much to say that every habit which a pupil exhibits is to be regarded as a reaction to stimuli which some persons or group of persons have presented to the child. It is not too much to say that the most important thing for the teacher to consider, as regards his present relations to his pupils, is the attitudes and habits which his own modes of being, saying, and doing are fostering or discouraging in them.

Now, if these two assumptions regarding educational psychology be granted, I think it will follow as a matter of course, that only by beginning with the values and laws contained in the student's own experience of his own mental growth, and by proceeding gradually to facts connected with other persons of whom he can know little; and by proceeding still more gradually to the attempt actually to influence the mental operations of others, can educational theory be made most effective. Only in this way can the most essential trait of the mental habit of the teacher be secured—that habit which looks upon the internal, not upon the external; which sees that the important function of the teacher is direction of the mental movement of the student, and that the mental movement must be known before it can be directed.

II. I turn now to the side of subject-matter, or scholarship, with the hope of showing that here too the material, when properly presented, is not so *merely* theoretical, remote from the practical problems of teaching, as is sometimes supposed. I recall that once a graduate student in a university made inquiries among all the leading teachers in the institution with which he was connected as to whether they had received any professional training, whether they had taken courses in pedagogy. The inquirer threw the results, which were mostly negative, into the camp of the local pedagogical club. Some may say that this proves nothing, because college teaching is proverbially poor, considered simply as teaching. Yet no one can deny that there is *some* good teaching, and some teaching of the very first order, done in colleges, and done by persons who have never had any instruction in either the theory or the practice of teaching.

This fact cannot be ignored any more than can the fact that there were good teachers before there was any such thing as pedagogy. Now, I am not arguing for not having pedagogical training—that is the last thing I want. But I claim the facts mentioned prove that scholarship *per se* may itself be a most effective tool for training and turning out good teachers. If it has accomplished so much when working unconsciously and without set intention, have we not good reason to believe that, when acquired in a training school for teachers—with the end of making teachers held definitely in view and with conscious reference to its relation to mental activity—it may prove a much more valuable pedagogical asset than we commonly consider it?

Scholastic knowledge is sometimes regarded as if it were something quite irrelevant to method. When this attitude is even unconsciously assumed, method becomes an external attachment to knowledge of subject-matter. It has to be elaborated and acquired in relative independence from subject-matter, and *then* applied.

Now the body of knowledge which constitutes the subject-matter of the student-teacher must, by the nature of the case, be organized subject-matter. It is not a miscellaneous heap of separate scraps. Even if (as in the case of history and literature), it be not technically termed "science," it is none the less material which has been subjected to method—has been selected and arranged with reference to controlling intellectual principles. There is, therefore, method in subject-matter itself—method indeed of the highest order which the human mind has yet evolved, scientific method.

It cannot be too strongly emphasized that this scientific method is the method of mind itself.[4] The classifications, interpretations, explanations, and generalizations which make subject-matter a branch of study do not lie externally in facts apart from mind. They reflect the attitudes and workings of mind in its endeavor to bring raw material of experience to a point where it at once satisfies and stimulates the needs of active thought. Such being the case, there is something wrong in the "academic" side of professional training, if by means of it the student does not constantly get object-lessons of the finest type in the kind of mental activity which characterizes mental growth and, hence, the educative process.

It is necessary to recognize the importance for the teacher's equipment of his own habituation to superior types of method of mental operation. The more a teacher in the future is likely to have to do with elementary teaching, the more, rather than the less, necessary is such exercise. Otherwise, the current traditions of elementary work with their tendency to talk and write down to the supposed intellectual level of children, will be likely to continue. Only a teacher thoroughly trained in the

[4] PROFESSOR ELLA F. YOUNG's "Scientific Method in Education" *(University of Chicago Decennial Publications)* is a noteworthy development of this conception, to which I am much indebted.

John Dewey

higher levels of intellectual method and who thus has constantly in his own mind a sense of what adequate and genuine intellectual activity means, will be likely, in deed, not in mere word, to respect the mental integrity and force of children.

Of course, this conception will be met by the argument that the scientific organization of subject-matter, which constitutes the academic studies of the student-teacher is upon such a radically different basis from that adapted to less mature students that too much pre-occupation with scholarship of an advanced order is likely actually to get in the way of the teacher of children and youth. I do not suppose anybody would contend that teachers really can know more than is good for them, but it may reasonably be argued that continuous study of a specialized sort forms mental habits likely to throw the older student out of sympathy with the type of mental impulses and habits which are found in younger persons.

Right here, however, I think normal schools and teachers' colleges have one of their greatest opportunities—an opportunity not merely as to teachers in training, but also for reforming methods of education in colleges and higher schools having nothing to do with the training of teachers. It is the business of normal schools and collegiate schools of education to present subject-matter in science, in language, in literature and the arts, in such a way that the student both sees and feels that these studies *are* significant embodiments of mental operations. He should be led to realize that they are not products of technical methods, which have been developed for the sake of the specialized branches of knowledge in which they are used, but represent fundamental mental attitudes and operations—that, indeed, particular scientific methods and classifications simply express and illustrate in their most concrete form that of which simple and common modes of thought-activity are capable when they work under satisfactory conditions.

In a word, it is the business of the "academic" instruction of future teachers to carry back subject-matter to its common psychical roots.[5] In so far as this is accomplished, the gap between the higher and the lower treatment of subject-matter, upon which the argument of the supposed objector depends, ceases to have the force which that argument assigns to it. This does not mean, of course, that exactly the same subject-matter, in the same mode of presentation, is suitable to a student in the elementary or high schools that is appropriate to the normal student. But it does mean that a mind which is habituated to viewing subject-matter from the standpoint of the function of that subject-matter in connection with *mental* responses, attitudes, and methods will be sensitive to *signs of intellectual activity* when exhibited in the child of four, or the youth of sixteen, and will be trained to a spontaneous and unconscious appreciation of the subject-matter which is fit to call out and direct mental activity.

We have here, I think, the explanation of the success of some teachers who violate every law known to and laid down by pedagogical science. They are themselves so full of the spirit of inquiry, so sensitive to every sign of its presence and absence, that no matter what they do, nor how they do it, they succeed in awakening and inspiring like alert and intense mental activity in those with whom they come in contact.

This is not a plea for the prevalence of these irregular, inchoate methods. But I feel that I may recur to my for-

[5] It is hardly necessary to refer to Dr. Harris's continued contention that normal training should give a higher view or synthesis of even the most elementary subjects.

mer remark: if some teachers, by sheer plenitude of knowledge, keep by instinct in touch with the mental activity of their pupils, and accomplish so much without, and even in spite of, principles which are theoretically sound, then there must be in this same scholarship a tremendous resource when it is more consciously used— that is, employed in clear connection with psychological principles.

When I said above that schools for training teachers have here an opportunity to react favorably upon general education, I meant that no instruction in subject-matter (wherever it is given) is adequate if it leaves the student with just acquisition of certain information about external facts and laws, or even a certain facility in the intellectual manipulation of this material. It is the business of our higher schools in all lines, and not simply of our normal schools, to furnish the student with the realization that, after all, it is the human mind, trained to effective control of its natural attitudes, impulses, and responses, that is the significant thing in all science and history and art so far as these are formulated for purposes of study.

The present divorce between scholarship and method is as harmful upon one side as upon the other—as detrimental to the best interests of higher academic instruction as it is to the training of teachers. But the only way in which this divorce can be broken down is by so presenting all subject-matter, for whatever ultimate, practical, or professional purpose, that it shall be apprehended as an objective embodiment of methods of mind in its search for, and transactions with, the truth of things.

Upon the more practical side, this principle requires that, so far as students appropriate new subject-matter (thereby improving their own scholarship and realizing more consciously the nature of method), they should finally proceed to organize this same subject-matter with reference to its use in teaching others. The curriculum of the elementary and the high school constituting the "practice" or "model" school ought to stand in the closest and most organic relation to the instruction in subject-matter which is given by the teachers of the professional school. If in any given school this is not the case, it is either because in the *training class* subject-matter is presented in an isolated way, instead of as a concrete expression of methods of mind, or else because the *practice school* is dominated by certain conventions and traditions regarding material and the methods of teaching it, and hence is not engaged in work of an adequate educational type.

As a matter of fact, as everybody knows, both of these causes contribute to the present state of things. On the one hand, inherited conditions impel the elementary school to a certain triviality and poverty of subject-matter, calling for mechanical drill, rather than for thought-activity, and the high school to a certain technical mastery of certain conventional culture subjects, taught as independent branches of the same tree of knowledge! On the other hand traditions of the different branches of science (the academic side of subject-matter) tend to subordinate the teaching in the normal school to the attainment of certain facilities, and the acquirement of certain information, both in greater or less isolation from their value as exciting and directing mental power.

The great need is convergence, concentration. Every step taken in the elementary and the high school toward intelligent introduction of more worthy and significant subject-matter, one requiring consequently for its assimilation thinking rather than "drill," must be met by a like advance step in which the mere isolated specialization of collegiate subject-matter is surrendered, and in which there is brought to conscious and interested attention its significance in expression of fundamental modes of mental activity—so fundamental as to be common to both the play of the mind upon the ordinary material of everyday experience and to the systematized material of the sciences.

III. As already suggested, this point requires that training students be exercised in making the connections between the course of study of the practice or model school, and the wider horizons of learning coming within their ken. But it is consecutive and systematic exercise in the consideration of the subject-matter of the elementary and high schools that is needed. The habit of making isolated and independent lesson plans for a few days' or weeks' instruction in a separate grade here or there not only does not answer this purpose, but is likely to be distinctly detrimental. Everything should be discouraged which tends to put the student in the attitude of snatching at the subject matter which he is acquiring in order to see if by some hook or crook it may be made immediately available for a lesson in this or that grade. What is needed is the habit of viewing the entire curriculum as a continuous growth, reflecting the growth of mind itself. This in turn demands, so far as I can see, consecutive and longitudinal consideration of the curriculum of the elementary and high school rather than a cross-sectional view of it. The student should be led to see that the same subject-matter in geography, nature-study, or art develops not merely day to day in a given grade, but from year to year throughout the entire movement of the school; and he should realize this before he gets much encouragement in trying to adapt subject-matter in lesson plans for this or that isolated grade.

C. If we attempt to gather together the points which have been brought out, we should have a view of practice work something like the following—though I am afraid even this formulates a scheme with more appearance of rigidity than is desirable:

At first, the practice school would be used mainly for purposes of observation. This observation, moreover, would not be for the sake of seeing how good teachers teach, or for getting "points" which may be employed in one's own teaching, but to get material for psychological observation and reflection, and some conception of the educational movement of the school as a whole.

Secondly, there would then be more intimate introduction to the lives of the children and the work of the school through the use as assistants of such students as had already got psychological insight and a good working acquaintance with educational problems. Students at this stage would not undertake much direct teaching, but would make themselves useful in helping the regular class instructor. There are multitudes of ways in which such help can be given and be of real help—that is, of use to the school, to the children, and not merely of putative value to the training student.[6] Special attention to backward children, to children who have been out of school, assisting in the care of material, in forms of hand-work, suggest some of the avenues of approach.

This kind of practical experience enables, in the third place, the future teacher to make the transition from his more psychological and theoretical insight to the observation of the more technical points of class teaching and management. The informality, gradualness, and famili-

[6] This question of some real need in the practice school itself for the work done is very important in its moral influence and in assimilating the conditions of "practice work" to those of real teaching.

arity of the earlier contact tend to store the mind with material which is unconsciously assimilated and organized, and thus supplies a background for work involving greater responsibility.

As a counterpart of this work in assisting, such students might well at the same time be employed in the selection and arrangement of subject-matter, as indicated in the previous discussion. Such organization would at the outset have reference to at least a group of grades, emphasizing continuous and consecutive growth. Later it might, without danger of undue narrowness, concern itself with finding supplementary materials and problems bearing upon the work in which the student is giving assistance; might elaborate material which could be used to carry the work still farther, if it were desirable; or, in case of the more advanced students, to build up a scheme of possible alternative subjects for lessons and studies.

Fourthly, as fast as students are prepared through their work of assisting for more responsible work, they could be given actual teaching to do. Upon the basis that the previous preparation has been adequate in subject-matter, in educational theory, and in the kind of observation and practice already discussed, such practice teachers should be given the maximum amount of liberty possible. They should not be too closely supervised, nor too minutely and immediately criticised upon either the matter or the method of their teaching. Students should be given to understand that they not only are *permitted* to act upon their own intellectual initiative, but that they are *expected* to do so, and that their ability to take hold of situations for themselves would be a more important factor in judging them than their following any particular set method or scheme.

Of course, there should be critical discussion with persons more expert of the work done, and of the educational results obtained. But sufficient time should be permitted to allow the practice-teacher to recover from the shocks incident to the newness of the situation, and also to get enough experience to make him capable of seeing the *fundamental* bearings of criticism upon work done. Moreover, the work of the expert or supervisor should be directed to getting the student to judge his own work critically, to find out for himself in what respects he has succeeded and in what failed, and to find the probable reasons for both failure and success, rather than to criticising him too definitely and specifically upon special features of his work.

It ought to go without saying (unfortunately, it does not in all cases) that criticism should be directed to making the professional student thoughtful about his work in the light of principles, rather than to induce in him a recognition that certain special methods are good, and certain other special methods bad. At all events, no greater travesty of real intellectual criticism can be given than to set a student to teaching a brief number of lessons, have him under inspection in practically all the time of every lesson, and then criticise him almost, if not quite, at the very end of each lesson, upon the particular way in which that particular lesson has been taught, pointing out elements of failure and of success. Such methods of criticism may be adapted to giving a training-teacher command of some of the knacks and tools of the trade, but are not calculated to develop a thoughtful and independent teacher.

Moreover, while such teaching (as already indicated) should be extensive or continuous enough to give the student time to become at home and to get a body of funded experience, it ought to be intensive in purpose rather than spread out miscellaneously. It is much more important for the teacher to assume responsibility for the consecutive development of some one topic, to get a feeling for the movement of that subject, than it is to teach a certain number (necessarily smaller in range) of lessons in a larger number of subjects. What we want, in other words, is not so much technical skill, as a realizing sense in the teacher of what the educational development of a subject means, and, in some typical case, command of a method of control, which will then serve as a standard for self-judgment in other cases.

Fifthly, if the practical conditions permit—if, that is to say, the time of the training course is sufficiently long, if the practice schools are sufficiently large to furnish the required number of children, and to afford actual demand for the work to be done—students who have gone through the stages already referred to should be ready for work of the distinctly apprenticeship type.

Nothing that I have said heretofore is to be understood as ruling out practice-teaching which is designed to give an individual mastery of the actual technique of teaching and management, provided school conditions permit it in reality and not merely in external form—provided, that is, the student has gone through a training in educational theory and history, in subject-matter, in observation, and in practice work of the laboratory type, before entering upon the latter. The teacher must acquire his technique some time or other; and if conditions are favorable, there are some advantages in having this acquisition take place in cadetting or in something of that kind. By means of this probation, persons who are unfit for teaching may be detected and eliminated more quickly than might otherwise be the case and before their cases have become institutionalized.

Even in this distinctly apprenticeship stage, however, it is still important that the student should be given as much responsibility and initiative as he is capable of taking, and hence that supervision should not be too unremitting and intimate, and criticism not at too short range or too detailed. The advantage of this intermediate probationary period does not reside in the fact that thereby supervisory officers may turn out teachers who will perpetuate their own notions and methods, but in the inspiration and enlightenment that come through prolonged contact with mature and sympathetic persons. If the conditions in the public schools were just what they ought to be, if all superintendents and principals had the knowledge and the wisdom which they should have, and if they had time and opportunity to utilize their knowledge and their wisdom in connection with the development of the younger teachers who come to them, the value of this apprenticeship period would be reduced, I think, very largely to its serving to catch in time and to exclude persons unfitted for teaching.

In conclusion, I may say that I do not believe that the principles presented in this paper call for anything utopian. The present movement in normal schools for improvement of range and quality of subject-matter is steady and irresistible. All the better classes of normal schools are already, in effect, what are termed "junior colleges." That is, they give two years' work which is almost, and in many cases quite, of regular college grade. More and more, their instructors are persons who have had the same kind of scholarly training that is expected of teachers in colleges. Many of these institutions are already of higher grade than this; and the next decade will certainly see a marked tendency on the part of many normal schools to claim the right to give regular collegiate bachelor degrees.

The type of scholarship contemplated in this paper is thus practically assured for the near future. If two other factors co-operate with this, there is no reason why the conception of relation of theory and practice here presented should not be carried out. The second necessary factor is that the elementary and high schools, which serve as schools of observation and practice, should represent an advanced type of education properly corresponding to the instruction in academic subject-matter and in educational theory given to the training classes. The third necessity is that work in psychology and educational theory make concrete and vital the connection between the normal instruction in subject-matter and the work of the elementary and high schools.

If it should prove impracticable to realize the conception herein set forth, it will not be, I think, because of any impossibility resident in the outward conditions, but because those in authority, both within and without the schools, believe that the true function of training schools is just to meet the needs of which people are already conscious. In this case, of course, training schools will be conducted simply with reference to perpetuating current types of educational practice, with simply incidental improvement in details.

The underlying assumption of this paper is, accordingly, that training schools for teachers do not perform their full duty in accepting and conforming to present educational standards, but that educational leadership is an indispensable part of their office. The thing needful is improvement of education, not simply by turning out teachers who can do better the things that are now necessary to do, but rather by changing the conception of what constitutes education.

7. Edward L. Thorndike: "The Contribution of Psychology to Education"*
(1910)

By the middle of the present century, it had become customary to describe John Dewey as the man who had reshaped American elementary and secondary schooling most fundamentally. Such a description had a certain validity if one looked only at public statements of what the modern American school sought to achieve. But if one examined curriculum guides, or considered the explanations classroom teachers gave for why they taught as they did, or reviewed the more commonly used criteria for selecting textbooks, he perceived that psychological terms, not philosophical propositions, dominated. American education was described in the language of social reform, but it was operated according to the language of psychology. And as far as elementary- and secondary-school men were concerned, the latter was largely the language of Edward L. Thorndike.

A similar phenomenon could be observed if one studied teacher education curricula: in the literature used in professional courses, each paragraph drawn essentially from Dewey was matched by several from Thorndike; each course in educational philosophy—and

* The Journal of Educational Psychology, I (January, 1910), 5–12.

history and sociology—was matched by two or three courses in educational psychology. The textbooks used for the latter courses, until the middle of the twentieth century, were generally those of Thorndike and his students. In short, American education and American teacher education had been "psychologized" under Thorndike's leadership.

The founding of The Journal of Educational Psychology both signified this tendency to "psychologize" education and contributed to it. That Thorndike was asked to write the keynote article reprinted below is significant: he had already become the symbol of the trend.

Psychology is the science of the intellects, characters and behavior of animals including man. Human education is concerned with certain changes in the intellects, characters and behavior of men, its problems being roughly included under these four topics: Aims, materials, means and methods.

Psychology contributes to a better understanding of the aims of education by defining them, making them clearer; by limiting them, showing us what can be done and what can not; and by suggesting new features that should be made parts of them.

Psychology makes ideas of educational aims clearer. When one says that the aim of education is culture, or discipline, or efficiency, or happiness, or utility, or knowledge, or skill, or the perfection of all one's powers, or development, one's statements, and probably one's thoughts, need definition. Different people, even amongst the clearest-headed of them, do not agree concerning just what culture is, or just what is useful. Psychology helps here by requiring us to put our notions of the aims of education into terms of the exact changes that education is to make, and by describing for us the changes which do actually occur in human beings.

Psychology helps to measure the probability that an aim is attainable. For example, certain writers about education state or imply that the knowledge and skill and habits of behavior which are taught to the children of today are of service not only to this generation and to later generations through the work this generation does, but also to later generations forever through the inheritance of increased capacity for knowledge and skill and morals. But if the mental and moral changes made in one generation are not transmitted by heredity to the next generation, the improvement of the race by direct transfer of acquisitions is a foolish, because futile aim.

Psychology enlarges and refines the aim of education. Certain features of human nature may be and have been thought to be unimportant or even quite valueless because of ignorance of psychology. Thus for hundreds of years in the history of certain races even the most gifted thinkers of the race have considered it beneath the dignity of education to make physical health an important aim. Bodily welfare was even thought of as a barrier to spiritual growth, an undesirable interferer with its proper master. Education aimed to teach it its proper place, to treat it as a stupid and brutish slave. It is partly because psychology has shown the world that the mind is the servant and co-worker as well as the master of the body, that the welfare of our minds and morals is intimately bound up with the welfare of our bodies, particularly of our central nervous systems, that today we can all see the eminence of bodily health as an aim of education.

To an understanding of the material of education, psychology is the chief contributor.

Edward L. Thorndike

Psychology shares with anatomy, physiology, sociology, anthropology, history and the other sciences that concern changes in man's bodily or mental nature the work of providing thinkers and workers in the field of education with knowledge of the material with which they work. Just as the science and art of agriculture depend upon chemistry and botany, so the art of education depends upon physiology and psychology.

A complete science of psychology would tell every fact about every one's intellect and character and behavior, would tell the cause of every change in human nature, would tell the result which every educational force —every act of every person that changed any other or the agent himself—would have. It would aid us to use human beings for the world's welfare with the same surety of the result that we now have when we use falling bodies or chemical elements. In proportion as we get such a science we shall become masters of our own souls as we now are masters of heat and light. Progress toward such a science is being made.

Psychology contributes to understanding of the means of education, first, because the intellects and characters of any one's parents, teachers and friends are very important means of educating him, and, second, because the influence of any other means, such as books, maps or apparatus, cannot be usefully studied apart from the human nature which they are to act upon.

Psychology contributes to knowledge of methods of teaching in three ways. First, methods may be deduced outright from the laws of human nature. For instance, we may infer from psychology that the difficulty pupils have in learning to divide by a fraction is due in large measure to the habit established by all the thousands of previous divisions which they have done or seen, the habit, that is, of "division—decrease" or "number divided—result smaller than the number." We may then devise or select such a method as will reduce this interference from the old habits to a minimum without weakening the old habits in their proper functioning.

Second, methods may be chosen from actual working experience, regardless of psychology, as a starting point. Thus it is believed that in the elementary school a class of fifteen pupils for one teacher gives better results than either a class of three or a class of thirty. Thus, also, it is believed that family life is better than institutional life in its effects upon character and enterprise. Thus, also, it is believed that in learning a foreign language the reading of simple discussions of simple topics is better than the translation of difficult literary masterpieces that treat subtle and complex topics. Even in such cases psychology may help by explaining *why* one method does succeed better and so leading the way to new insights regarding other questions not yet settled by experience.

Third, in all cases psychology, by its methods of measuring knowledge and skill, may suggest means to test and verify or refute the claims of any method. For instance, there has been a failure on the part of teachers to decide from their classroom experience whether it is better to teach the spelling of a pair of homonyms together or apart in time. But all that is required to decide the question for any given pair is for enough teachers to use both methods with enough different classes, keeping everything else except the method constant, and to measure the errors in spelling the words thereafter in the two cases. Psychology, which teaches us how to measure changes in human nature, teaches us how to decide just what the results of any method of teaching are.

So far I have outlined the contribution of psychology to education from the point of view of the latter's problems. I shall now outline very briefly the work being done by psychologists which is of special significance to the theory and practice of education and which may be expected to result in the largest and most frequent contributions.

It will, of course, be understood that directly or indirectly, soon or late, every advance in the sciences of human nature will contribute to our success in controlling human nature and changing it to the advantage of the common weal. If certain lines of work by psychologists are selected for mention here, it is only because they are the more obvious, more direct and, so far as can now be seen, greater aids to correct thinking about education.

The first line of work concerns the discovery and improvement of means of measurement of intellectual functions. (The study of means of measuring moral functions such as prudence, readiness to sacrifice an immediate for a later good, sympathy, and the like, has only barely begun.) Beginning with easy cases such as the discrimination of sensory differences, psychology has progressed to measuring memory and accuracy of movement, fatigue, improvement with practice, power of observing small details, the quantity, rapidity and usefulness of associations, and even to measuring so complex a function as general intelligence and so subtle a one as suggestibility.

The task of students of physical science in discovering the thermometer, galvanometer and spectroscope, and in defining the volt, calorie, erg, and ampère, is being attempted by psychologists in the sphere of human nature and behavior. How important such work is to education should be obvious. At least three-fourths of the problems of educational practice are problems whose solution depends upon the *amount* of some change in boys and girls. Of two methods, which gives the *greater* skill? Is the gain in general ability from a "disciplinary" study so great as to outweigh the loss in specially useful habits? Just how much more does a boy learn when thirty dollars a year is spent for his teaching than when only twenty dollars is spent? Units in which to measure the changes wrought by education are essential to an adequate science of education. And, though the students of education may establish these units by their own investigations, they can use and will need all the experience of psychologists in the search for similar units.

The second line of work concerns race, sex, age and individual differences in all the many elements of intellect and character and behavior.

How do the Igorottes, Ainus, Japanese and Esquimaux differ in their efficiency in learning to operate certain mechanical contrivances? Is the male sex more variable than the female in mental functions? What happens to keenness of sensory discrimination with age? How do individuals of the same race, sex and age differ in efficiency in perceiving small visual details or in accuracy in equaling a given length, or in the rapidity of movement? These are samples of many questions which psychologists have tried to answer by appropriate measurements. Such knowledge of the differences which exist amongst men for whatever reason is of service to the thinker about the particular differences which education aims to produce between a man and his former self.

These studies of individual differences or variability are being supplemented by studies of correlations. How far does superior vividness and fidelity in imagery from one sense go with inferiority in other sorts of imagery? To what extent is motor ability a symptom of intellectual ability? Does the quick learner soon forget? What are the mental types that result from the individual variations in mental functions and their inter-correlations? Psychology has already determined with more or less surety the answers to a number of such questions instructive in their bearing upon both scientific insight into human nature and practical arrangements for controlling it.

The extent to which the intellectual and moral differences found in human beings are consequences of their original nature and determined by the ancestry from which they spring, is a matter of fundamental importance for education. So also is the manner in which ancestral influence operates. Whether such qualities as leadership, the artistic temperament, originality, persistence, mathematical ability, or motor skill are represented in the germs each by one or a few unit characters so that they "Mendelize" in inheritance, or whether they are represented each by the coöperation of so many unit characters that the laws of their inheritance are those of "blending" is a question whose answer will decide in great measure the means to be employed for racial improvement. Obviously both the amount and the mode of operation of ancestral influence upon intellect and character are questions which psychology should and does investigate.

The results and methods of action of the many forces which operate in childhood and throughout life to change a man's original nature are subjects for study equally appropriate to the work of a psychologist, a sociologist or a student of education, but the last two will naturally avail themselves of all that the first achieves. Although as yet the studies of such problems are crude, speculative and often misguided, we may hope that the influence of climate, food, city life, the specialization of industry, the various forms of the family and of the state, the different "studies" of the schools, and the like will come to be studied by as careful psychologists and with as much care as is now the case with color-vision or the perception of distance.

The foundation upon which education builds is the equipment of instincts and capacity given by nature apart from training. Just as knowledge of the peculiar inheritance characteristic of any individual is necessary to efficient treatment of him, so knowledge of the unlearned tendencies of man as a species is necessary to efficient planning for education in general. Partly in conscious response to this demand and partly as a result of growing interest in comparative and genetic psychology, there have been in the last two decades many studies by psychologists of both the general laws of instinct and their particular natures, dates of appearance and disappearance, and conditions of modifiability. The instincts of attitude—of interest and aversion—are of course to be included here, as well as the tendencies to more obviously effective responses.

It is unfortunately true that the unlearned tendencies to respond of ants and chickens have been studied with more care than those of men, and also that the extreme complexity and intimate mixture with habits in the case of human instincts prevent studies of them, even when made with great care, from giving entirely unambiguous and elegant results. But the educational theorist or practitioner who should conclude that his casual observations of children in homes and schools need no reinforcement from the researches of psychologists would be making the same sort of, though not so great, an error as the pathologist or physician who should neglect the scientific studies of bacteria and protozoa. Also the psychologist who condemns these studies *in toto* because they lack the precision and surety of his own studies of sensations and perceptual judgments is equally narrow, though from a better motive.

The modifications of instincts and capacities into habits and powers and the development of the latter are the subjects of researches in dynamic psychology which are replacing the vague verbal and trite maxims of what used to be called "applied psychology" by definite insights into reality far in advance of those which common-sense sagacity alone can make. We are finding out when and why "practice makes perfect" and when and why it does not; wherein the reinforcement of a connection between situation and response by resulting satisfaction is better than the inhibition of alternative connections by discomfort and wherein it is not; what the law of diminishing returns from equal amounts of practice is, what it implies, and how it is itself limited; how far the feelings of achievement, of failure and of fatigue are symptomatic of progress, retardation and unfitness for work. Such a list of topics could be much extended even now and is being increased rapidly as more psychologists and more gifted psychologists come to share in the study of the learning process.

Only twenty years ago a student could do little more than add to his own common-sense deductions from the common facts of life the ordered series of similar deductions by the sagacious Bain. Bain utilized all the psychology of his day as well as the common fund of school-room experience, but today his book is hopelessly outgrown. Although it was the source of the minor books on the topic during the eighties and nineties, no one would now think of presenting the facts of the science of education by a revised edition of Bain.

Other lines of psychological work deserve more than mention. Incidental contributions from studies of sensory and perceptual processes, imagery and memory, attention and distraction, facilitation, inhibition and fatigue, imitation and suggestion, the rate and accuracy of movement and other topics—even from studies made with little or no concern about the practical control of human nature—sum up to a body of facts which do extend and economize that control. The special psychology of babies, children and adolescents is obviously important to education. False infant psychology or false child psychology is harmful, not because it is infant psychology, but because it is false.

I give only mention to these so as to save space in which to call attention to another relation between psychology and education which is not sufficiently known. The science of education can and will itself contribute abundantly to psychology. Not only do the laws derived by psychology from simple, specially arranged experiments help us to interpret and control mental action under the conditions of school-room life. School-room life itself is a vast laboratory in which are made thousands of experiments of the utmost interest to "pure" psychology. Not only does psychology help us to understand the mistakes made by children in arithmetic. These mistakes afford most desirable material for studies of the action of the laws of association, analysis and selective thinking. Experts in education studying the responses to school situations for the sake of practical control will advance knowledge not only of the mind as a learner under school conditions but also of the mind for every point of view.

Indeed I venture to predict that this journal will before many years contain a notable proportion of articles reporting answers to psychological questions got from the facts of educational experience, in addition to its list of papers reporting answers to educational questions got from the experiments of the laboratory.

All that is here written may seem very obvious and needless, and meet the tragic fate of being agreed with by every one who reads it. I hope that it is obvious and needless, and that the relation between psychology and education is not, in the mind of any competent thinker, in any way an exception to the general case that action in the world should be guided by the truth about the world; and that any truth about it will directly or indirectly, soon or late, benefit action.

8. William S. Learned, William C. Bagley, *et al.*: "Purpose of a Normal School"*

(1920)

In 1914, Governor Elliott W. Major of Missouri obtained the support of the Carnegie Foundation for a study of the teacher education problems of his state. In organizing the study, William S. Learned, of the Foundation's staff, enlisted the services of people who were, or were destined to become, shapers of "professional" thought about American education. Among them were: William C. Bagley of Teachers College, Columbia University, whose students established the field of teacher education as an area of specialized scholarship; Charles A. McMurry of Illinois Normal University, George Peabody College for Teachers, and Teachers College, an expert on "methods of instruction" who had led the early Herbartian movement in America; Ned Dearborn of Harvard University, one of the early advocates of scientific measurement in education; and George D. Strayer of Teachers College, who perhaps as much as any one man made the school survey a permanent feature of American life.

* *The Professional Preparation of Teachers for American Public Schools: A Study Based upon an Examination of Tax-Supported Normal Schools in the State of Missouri*, Carnegie Foundation for the Advancement of Teaching, Bulletin No. 14 (New York: The Foundation, 1920), pp. 70–82.

Missouri was their laboratory, the nation their audience. Their survey was the first of several massive studies of American teacher education. Paradoxically, though their techniques represented the wave of the future, their basic values and assumptions were quickly to wane. In no subsequent major study will be found so complete a consensus in favor of the single-purpose teachers college.

A. GENERAL FUNCTION

1. THE EXISTING CONCEPTION

"What should a normal school be?" This is a question which, according to Joseph Baldwin, the first president at Kirksville, "only the angels can answer." Whatever the accuracy of this verdict, it is possible at least to discover what the function of the institution has been as worked out in practice in Missouri.

EARLY CONCEPTION OF THE FUNCTION OF A NORMAL SCHOOL

The question may be reduced to the following alternatives: the normal school shall either provide a general education, making its professional features more or less incidental, or it shall undertake to give an intensive professional training, exclusively for teachers. Of these alternatives, Missouri at any time in her early normal school history would have emphatically asserted the latter. From the beginning, the movement was in the hands of men who had unlimited faith in the professional idea. Its appeal was founded on the prevailing low state of training among common school teachers, and it was promoted by teachers, superintendents, and associations of these, who had definitely in mind the elevation of the class as a whole. So in 1871 the State Teachers Association at Chillicothe resolved "that the normal schools should be at the head of our educational system; that the course should be purely professional; and that all prepartory work should be done in the public schools and universities."[1] The early curricula exhibit this predominant idea very clearly: it was never a question of giving or of not giving the professional subjects, but always of how much academic material would suffice to supplement the defective preparation with which most students came equipped. All subjects were presented or reviewed from the standpoint of their most effective presentation to a class, and the practical usages of instruction received heavy emphasis. "No effort has been spared to make the institution exclusively a school for teachers."[2] "In arranging the course of instruction strict regard has been paid to the requirements of the public schools of Missouri, and in carrying out that course our constant aim has been to give such training as will best qualify the graduate both intellectually and morally for effective work as a teacher."[3] These statements from Warrensburg in 1878 and 1886 reveal the attitude of the other schools as well. President Baldwin, at Kirksville, declared in 1872 that "every energy is directed to preparing for the public schools of Missouri the largest number of good teachers in the shortest time,"[4] and in 1880: the aim of the school is "to give culture and learning, not for the

[1] *Report of the Superintendent of Public Schools,* 1871, page 19.
[2] *Ibid.,* 1878, page 224.
[3] *Ibid.,* 1886, page 108.
[4] *Ibid.,* 1872, page 166.

benefit of the student, but that it may be used in the education of the masses."[5] Especially instructive are the observations of State Superintendent Monteith, who was in office when the schools were started:

> It is a pretty well-defined result of experience, too, that normal schools should be quite elementary in respect to the subject matter and curriculum of study. In a school system which embraces high schools and universities, there is not the slightest reason why the normal school should duplicate the instruction of these more advanced institutions. I am thoroughly convinced, in observing the mistakes of other states, that the normal school is disappointing the object of its design when it drifts away from the common schools of the country. With this object steadily in view, our Board of Regents are endeavoring to adjust the two schools already established to the special conditions and wants of the state. The higher mathematics and dead languages, except within a certain eminently practical limit, are to give way to a more generous attention to natural science, drawing, and the perfecting of teachers in the best methods of conducting the common branches of the common school.[6]

Missouri normal schools, therefore, were founded to train teachers. To say "exclusively" would be technically wrong, as certain readjustments were occasionally made here and there; for example, special classes in Greek were sometimes offered to accommodate a few who wished to go to the university, and certain individuals were occasionally present who did not declare their intention to teach. But the clear and consistent aim apparent under all circumstances was to provide teachers, actual or prospective, with special skill for their duties, and in their reports to the legislature all the schools were solicitous to show that the largest possible proportion of their students were actually teaching in the state.

[5] *Ibid.*, 1880, page 159.
[6] *Ibid.*, 1872, page 37.

SUBSEQUENT VARIATIONS

This fixed purpose of the first thirty years has wavered in some schools during the subsequent period. The three original institutions furnish an interesting contrast in this respect. In 1909, under the caption "People's College," Kirksville announced itself as follows:

The State Normal School, Kirksville, Mo., is attempting to do a great work for the people of the state by giving studies reaching from the kindergarten through the most advanced college courses. This wide range of work—meeting the demands of all the people—is found in very few first class schools. While advanced common school courses are given in this institution for the benefit of those who are preparing to teach in the rural and ungraded schools, academic degrees are conferred upon those who have completed the work offered by our best colleges. This brings the school in close touch with the people by giving an elaborate education to those who want to enter the professions, and a vocational education for those who want to take practical business courses. It cannot be denied that the Normal School comes nearer the people than other schools and may therefore be justly called the People's College.[7]

This statement is followed by an extensive program of courses that are clearly not intended for teachers—one-year curricula chiefly in farming and commerce. Nowhere in this bulletin, furthermore, is there a clear statement that the school is of a limited professional character, or that a declaration of intention to teach is required. It holds out rather an alluring vision of a sort of educational lunch counter where everything "the people" wish may be had in portions suited to their convenience.

The "People's College" idea does not appear to have thrived; at any rate, nothing more is heard of it, and the catalogue of the following year goes back plainly to the

[7] *Bulletin* (Supplement), *Kirksville*, June, 1909, page 1.

original aim: "The Normal School is not a college for general culture. It is a vocational institution of college rank. Under the law its students declare their intention to teach in the public schools." The subsequent catalogues have shown a single, strong professional purpose.

At Cape Girardeau an enlargement of scope was announced in the same year as at Kirksville. The catalogue of 1909 declares: "The Normal School has a larger mission in Southeast Missouri than that of a state college for teachers.... The institution must be to this section of the state their one great college. It is fully equipped to meet the demands that are naturally made upon it. In its college courses; in its agricultural courses; in its Manual Training School; in its domestic science and domestic art courses; in its School of Music; in its business courses; and in its teachers' college the people of Southeast Missouri will find the opportunity to educate themselves for their life work."

Tho placing its teachers college last in the above list, the school elsewhere in the catalogue clearly defines its legal teacher-training function as a portion of its activity. In the catalogue of 1910 its "Field of Service" is formally described as comprising "A School for Teachers," a "Subcollegiate" department, and "A State College," the latter offering (since 1907) courses leading to the degree of A.B. and requiring in them no work in education whatever. Here we have, therefore, an institution deliberately revising its organization throughout and introducing, not one-year vocational courses as at Kirksville, but an elaborate curriculum with a new and alien purpose. It is difficult to see how either school could reconcile these departures with the law's demand for an exaction from each student of a declaration of intention to teach in the schools of Missouri. Cape Girardeau, and possibly Kirksville, has been saved from embarrassment thru the fact that but for a single case no graduate has taken the courses except prospective teachers who could also avow their intention to teach; that, however, scarcely justifies the appeal for students distinctly excluded by law. This divided purpose at Cape Girardeau has never been abandoned. On the contrary, it has been officially reaffirmed in the school's magazine publications of 1913 and 1914,[8] where the pledge to teach is declared to be out of date, and it is frankly proposed to adapt the institution to the needs of men and women who will teach but a short time, if at all, and whose professional interest is therefore incidental at best.

Warrensburg, on the other hand, has consistently adhered to the original plan, to the extent, at least, of an unequivocal announcement of her special aim in every catalogue down to the present year. An expression in the school's biennial report of 1885 is a fair sample of the early attitude: "On all proper occasions we have taken pains to spread abroad the impression that this school is designed for the training of teachers and for no other purpose whatever." In the catalogue of 1904 the "Object of the School" is defined in the following paragraphs:

In the law creating Normal Schools in this State the following passages occur:

"The course of instruction shall be confined to such branches of science only as are usually taught in Normal Schools and which may be necessary to qualify the students as competent teachers in the public schools of this State.

"Every applicant for admission shall undergo an examination in such manner as may be prescribed by the Board [of Regents], and they shall require the applicant to sign and file with the Secretary of the Board a declaration of intention to follow the business of teaching in the public schools of this State."

[8] *The Educational Outlook*, October, 1913, page 136.

The following is the pledge required of every student upon entrance and registration:

"I hereby declare that it is my intention to follow the business of teaching in the public schools of this State, and that I voluntarily enroll myself as a student in the State Normal School at Warrensburg for the purpose of preparing for that work."

The limits prescribed for the course of study and the form of the pledge show that but one purpose was contemplated by the State in establishing these schools, viz.: *The training of teachers* for the public schools of the State.[9]

Similarly in 1905 and after, the school's "sole function is the preparation of teachers for the schools of Missouri." "The school does not exist for the benefit of its students, but for the benefit of the whole people."[10] And in 1912: The school's "sole purpose is to confer on its students that education, discipline, professional training, and practical skill which will best fit them for teaching in the public schools of the State."[11]

The schools at Springfield and Maryville, founded in 1906, have in general followed the exclusively professional ideal also, as their catalogues attest. Southwest Missouri has been an unusually fruitful field for such single-minded service, and the school at Springfield has prospered remarkably. Maryville, in 1914, devotes two pages of its catalogue to the exposition of this distinctly professional aim. It is with some surprise, therefore, that one sees it weakened in 1916. The school now calls itself simply "an educational institution," and, besides enumerating the various teacher-groups that are provided for, invites also those who are "seeking to secure the preliminary college academic requirement" for the university, or students from other colleges who seek "to extend their credits in college," and finally observes "that many per-

[9] *Catalogue, Warrensburg,* 1904, page 15.
[10] *Ibid.,* 1905, page 20.
[11] *Ibid.,* 1912, page 16.

sons not immediately concerned with teaching find pleasure and profit in becoming enrolled in our classes." There is no reference to the declaration of intention to teach required by law.

SPECIAL CONSIDERATIONS AFFECTING A NORMAL SCHOOL'S CONCEPTION OF ITS FUNCTION

Before discussing the merits of the question involved in these divergent proposals, there are certain additional facts to be considered. In spite of the professional ideal that, with the above exceptions, has dominated the schools, the notion of a general education has almost unconsciously, and for historical reasons, influenced their purpose. From the beginning the students in these normal schools have been exceedingly heterogeneous, with a preponderance of mature minds of good ability but with very defective preparation due to lack of opportunity. The all-important preliminary process was therefore necessarily one of fundamental education, and it is impressive to note how consistently the Missouri normal schools have urged this principle, even tho at times they appear to have failed to practise it. Throughout their history they seem to have been ardent advocates of having something to teach as compared with certain schools in other states that sacrificed their character on the altar of "method."

PRESSURE FOR ACADEMIC CREDIT

Furthermore, it should be noted that as purveyors to that occupation of teaching whereby chiefly needy and ambitious boys and girls obtained the means for further education, these institutions stood in tempting relation to the fuller education that their students sought. It was a matter of course that the kind of student who came to the normal school had taught or would teach; teaching was his most obvious resource for temporary support. Hence in very many cases the student accepted professional work as a necessary incident, while his real attention was upon the academic work that would be accepted for credit in another and higher institution. It was but a step, and a very natural step, for the normal school to develop its requirements with such an end in view. A genuine desire to prove serviceable to hard-working students who were using the teaching profession merely as a ladder, and a less worthy feeling that such students brought to the school not only numbers but prestige, combined to enhance the "college" idea as a legitimate goal. Aside from Cape Girardeau's wholly non-professional curriculum already mentioned, the sixty-hour curriculum for high school graduates at Maryville, in 1914, illustrates such a purpose: in the effort to offer only subjects that might be used for credit elsewhere, no special study of the history, geography, and arithmetic that these students were presumably later to teach was required, except as it appeared fragmentarily in ten semester hours of practice teaching.[12]

That pressure of this sort has been and still continues to be severe seems evident from the replies made by students to enquiries at the various schools. Sixty per cent of the students in attendance at the time of inspection declared that they did not intend to teach permanently. With the women the factor of prospective marriage probably weighs heavily; this cannot, however, be true of

[12] Good normal schools elsewhere were at the same time requiring 12–15 semester hours in these subjects aside from a full semester of practice work.

the men, seventy-eight per cent of whom make the negative reply. Such students naturally have little interest in an intensive professional training; those studies please them best which give them the most credit for future use. Even the men who are intending to continue in the field of education find but little inducement in the work properly expected from most of the women. The latter expect to teach, while the men hope to go directly into administrative positions. As a group the men in the normal schools seem to be a disintegrating element, yet the efforts made to attract and retain them indicate that their presence is nevertheless much preferred to a homogeneous professional group more largely made up of women.

EFFECT OF LOCAL CONTROL

A third motive for stress on general education has arisen from the complete local attachment and control of the schools. The town or county has paid a heavy bonus for the location, and naturally exercises proprietorship. The schools are severally in the hands of local boards, who really own them in behalf of their respective districts. They are maintained largely, to be sure, out of state funds, but the amount of such appropriations depends upon the energy and influence of their board members and friends who lobby vigorously, and is never in any sense the considered proposal of a state authority directing the institution solely for the good of the whole state. They become, therefore, the local public educational institutions; and the fundamental theory of a school to train public servants for the benefit of the state is largely obscured by the more attractive idea of a place where local youth may prepare for college, or even pursue collegiate studies and acquire degrees. Town or sectional pride urges this interpretation on the institution, which in turn is anxious to recruit its numbers because of its feeling of responsibility to the local community.[13] Regents with pet notions find an easy field of influence, and often have slight perception of the larger purpose of the school. One of these urged that, as his school had an old telescope in its possession, it should undertake collegiate courses in astronomy. Administrators naturally yield most quickly to the forces that feed and affect the school, and when dependent solely upon such local influences can scarcely be blamed if truer ideals seem distant and impracticable. It is easy, under these circumstances, to *include* the professional idea, because, as already pointed out, it fits the economic situation of most of the student patrons; but to make it really the sole and sufficient reason for the school's existence is less easy, and probably cannot be fully accomplished under the present system of control.

"DEMOCRACY" THE JUSTIFICATION

The situation described in the foregoing paragraph has, of course, developed a theory, or the interpretation of a theory, for its justification. Great emphasis is placed on the perfectly valid creed that the people know what they want, and that democracy in education consists in grati-

[13] An everywhere vigorous and vocal expression of this town pride rises from the vested interests dependent on the schools—boarding-houses, stores, churches, and so on. Thus, a writer in the local newspaper of one of the normal school towns struck a responsive chord when he declared that the present study would undoubtedly discourage the attendance of men at the school, and send both men and women to "enrich the boarding houses of some other place." *Kirksville Express,* December 10, 1914.

fying their desires. But from this creed there is then drawn the inference that because the people desire good teachers, the people are therefore competent to direct the institution that provides them, and that the institution is most "democratic" that yields itself most completely to the popular local fancy. Such, unfortunately, are the terms on which it is often possible, thru spectacular features, to develop a large school; but such is not the way to give the people what they, at heart, desire. An intelligent society has learned not to interfere with competent professional service when it would be healed or seek justice at court; that service commands the maximum confidence which, for a selected end, most completely refines and dominates its choice of means. This temper is superlatively characteristic of a good school; it must mould and dominate public opinion in its field; it must guard its aims and processes from public interference precisely in order that the public may get the service that it wants. No other interpretation of public service is worthy of a democracy, but the present system of local control makes such detached and efficient service difficult if not impossible.

PROFESSIONAL TRAINING LONG UNCERTAIN AS TO ITS METHOD

Finally, the development of professional training itself has involved the conception of general education in an ambiguous and confusing manner. When the Missouri normal schools were established, two theories existed as to their operation. According to the first, the purpose of the schools should be solely to teach subject-matter properly; it was said that students would teach precisely as they had been taught, and could shift for themselves if filled with ideas to be communicated. According to the second theory, only the indispensable subject-matter should be given; the main purpose should be to develop the philosophy of method and to test the skill of the candidate in using methods. The latter theory was the one adopted and chiefly followed,[14] altho, as has been said, the schools appear to have insisted usually that the foundation of subject-matter should be substantial. Little by little, however, both in Missouri and elsewhere, the whole normal school practice seems to have hardened into a formalized method from which the schools were aroused thru criticism by the universities. The latter had been persistent adherents of the first of the two doctrines noted; consequently the cult of "method" received little but ridicule, and in so far as it had developed a pose to hide its insufficient learning, its pretensions were quickly punctured. Under the fire of this attack many unworthy accretions of "professional" lore disappeared—sentimentalism, mystic reverence for formulae, a not infrequent quackery; while such conceptions as survived the refining process were eventually accepted for use in normal school and university alike.

Apart from this salutary process, however, and somewhat preceding it, came an increased mechanical emphasis on what the university primarily stood for, namely, content. In Missouri this is illustrated by the change that came over all the institutions about 1900, when within two years the headship in each was transferred to a new man. The university high school inspector and former state superintendent of public schools went to Kirksville with a commission from the president of the university to "go and put scholarship into that school." The presi-

[14] These two points of view are well stated in one of Superintendent Monteith's discussions. See *State Report*, 1872, page 37.

dent of Central College at Fayette, Missouri, went to Warrensburg, and a successful school superintendent, a graduate of the state university, went to Cape Girardeau. The effect of this infusion of fresh academic blood became immediately apparent in the announcements of the schools: the cultural idea; the proposal, in order to make teachers, to make "first educated men and women;" the notion of "a broad academic foundation" are all insistently emphasized. Accordingly, the studies considered "academic" were set off sharply from those termed "professional," and commanded a certain special respect if only because they were terms shared in common with the higher academic world; and this distinction has in general been pronounced even to the present day.

The influence of this development has been marked both on the students and on the institutions. In effect the school has unconsciously said to the student: "This academic foundation is your education; it is of prime importance, it has nothing to do with teaching, it is what you want for life, it will serve you if you proceed to college or professional school; as a teacher-preparing agency we are obliged to hang in your belt certain tools that will get you a license and may be useful if you teach, but they are not big enough to be in the way if you do not, and an educated person ought to have them anyhow." Thus its very endeavors to meet more satisfactorily its professional purpose by strengthening the academic foundation have created in the normal school a divided aim which it has not known how to unify, and of which the various other centrifugal tendencies already enumerated have taken full advantage.

In its effect upon the institution itself this situation has been positively disastrous. With the emphatic division of subjects into academic and professional groups came naturally a corresponding division of the staff. Teachers of educational subjects, including the practice-school director and supervisors, should be the core of the institution; distinct from them are the academic instructors, who generally will have nothing to do with the practice school or its works. In members of the academic staff, pride of subject, and often of better training, has bred not a little scorn (carried over, perhaps, from the universities from whence they came) for the department of "pedagogy" and the ill-paid supervisors of the training school. At any rate, these academic instructors have rarely been selected for their knowledge of how to teach young children; their interests and sympathies are elsewhere, and the organization of the school has usually failed to exact of them responsibility for this phase of their duty.

In some normal schools, not in Missouri, the faculty is split from top to bottom on this line, and even in Missouri, with the sole exception of Springfield, the cleavage is apparent. The inevitable tendency of such division of sympathy and purpose is to reproduce itself in the mind of the student. His strictly educational courses lack conviction because they lack relation, and fail of the illustrative and cumulative force latent in the so-called "content" subjects; the latter, in turn, conceived as ends in themselves for "general education," terminate often in a series of blind alleys whence the student neither gets further nor sees how his achievement affects his main purpose.

2. Normal Schools Should Train Teachers

It is the judgment of the authors of this report that institutions established by the state to prepare teachers as public servants for its schools should make that business their sole purpose and concern. The character of such preparation is a question of administrative knowledge and policy. It will depend upon the amount of financial support available, and will be modified by the varying need for teachers in the state and by the rewards offered in the communities to be served. But with their method and specific goal thus defined, no consideration whatever should divert such schools from their task.

The grounds for this conclusion are simple and obvious. The question is one of institutional economy. Each school has a certain amount of energy expressed in terms of its annual appropriation plus its organization and permanent plant. With this energy it confronts a definite and difficult task contemplated in the statute,[15] namely, with the help of four similar schools and of the university, to place a competent teacher in every teaching position in the state. This is a task with which these six schools have scarcely begun to cope. It is a task so great that large and important portions of it have temporarily to be farmed out, as in the inevitable allotment for the present of the teachers of the large cities to the city training schools, and of rural teachers to the high school training classes. Hitherto the schools have trained a few teachers thoroughly, and have given a meagre smattering to a vast number. Even the few have received a generalized training which will not be tolerable longer if the reasonable

[15] The Revised Statutes of 1909 declare that "the course of instruction in each normal school shall be confined to such subjects in the sciences and arts as are usually taught in normal schools and necessary to qualify the students to become competent teachers in the public schools." See Chap. 106, Art. 14, Sect. 11071. An Act of 1919 extends this to include "such subjects in the arts and sciences as are usually taught in teachers' colleges, normal schools or schools of education." Sect. 11075.

demands of educated communities are to be met in Missouri as they are already met in some other states. There is an overwhelming need for more prolonged and more intensive training, extended to include as many as can be reached. In the face of this heavy obligation which the state lays upon the normal schools, it is difficult to justify the proposal of any school, say of Cape Girardeau, to use its share of the all too scanty training funds to develop a local university. This means, as indicated in the prospectus already quoted, to relegate its training of teachers to an inconspicuous department; to promote the other phases of collegiate work for their own sake and not alone as they produce better teachers; to fill classes, as college classes are now filled, with some who will teach, some who will farm, some who will be politicians, and many who have no specific purpose; in other words, to sacrifice the enormous advantage of momentum and *morale* that inheres in a single fine idea well worked out, for a round of inevitable mediocrity. For the school has at best wholly insufficient funds for its present logical purpose—the preparation of a competent teacher for every position in its district. To take over other projects, as these are conceived in modern education, is not only to fail in its proper task but to fail altogether.

The case of Cape Girardeau is especially interesting, inasmuch as for many years both regents and administration have made every effort to realize this "larger" notion. Elaborate advanced "college" curricula, special scholarships "for graduates from other colleges," and an enthusiastic literature have all pushed the idea. But only a single graduate has as yet (1917) gone out from such courses; the school is still as solely a normal school as is any of the other four. And with good reason: Cape Girardeau has taken pride in being a good school, and both teachers and students have dimly perceived that it was impossible to be a good normal school and a "great college" on the same appropriation. There is doubtless truth in the claim that, as college attendance is in great part local, more southeast Missourians would go to college if they had one nearby. But it is just as true that a good normal school is a professional school throughout and cannot be an arts college; if it wishes to conduct a college that is self-respecting, it must have double funds, separate classes, another faculty selected for that purpose, and so on. The combination is not a happy one in any place where it is now on trial, and the logic both of theory and experience is against it. The college agitation at Cape Girardeau has probably done good rather than harm; some public interest has been aroused, and a college foundation may some time seize the imagination of the wealthy men of that region or be developed from the local high school by way of a junior college as elsewhere in Missouri; but the obvious way to help in bringing about this result is for the present institution to discharge its own peculiar task well, and to fix its ambitions on becoming the best purely professional training school for teachers in the Middle West.

Cape Girardeau is an excellent illustration of a school-appropriated body and soul by the local community in the hope of making it the engine of local ambitions. The town and county bought the school in the first place, and can scarcely be blamed for owning it now. Fortunately state control of the funds, by forcing it into comparison with the other schools, still determines its general line of action, but it can probably never reach its maximum power until it acquires a controlling board disentangled from local concerns and sympathetic with its proper purpose. Reimbursement of this and the other counties for their original outlay would be a small price to pay as compared with the benefit of independent management.

OBSTACLES TO PROFESSIONAL TRAINING ARE DISAPPEARING

Other obstacles to an exclusive and intensive professional development in normal schools are happily vanishing. Secondary work, to which the normal schools have hitherto of necessity been tied, seems destined early to disappear from them. The phenomenal increase in high school facilities has brought secondary education within the possible reach of nearly every student,[16] and the higher institution owes it to the lower to turn back every pupil of high school age who can attend a local or neighboring school before coming to the normal school. Many of these country high schools have large contingents who come in for the week from the surrounding territory. Especially where training classes are installed, every consideration appears to favor the development of local training centres for secondary work. Mature persons, for whom the high school makes unsatisfactory provision, should be given opportunities elsewhere.[17]

The question of relation with other higher institutions is likewise being disposed of successfully. As this problem has existed, however, an important distinction should be made clear. It is one thing for those who have taken a strictly professional course and who expect to give themselves seriously to teaching to urge that they be allowed

[16] See William S. Learned, William C. Bagley, *et al.*, *The Professional Preparation of Teachers for American Public Schools*, page 297.
[17] See *ibid.*, page 300.

to continue their preparation in other institutions without loss of credit; it is quite another thing for persons who have no such intention to demand that the normal school give them a general education that will see them into college and professional school. For the first group adjustment has already been accomplished. Two-year graduates of the normal school may enter the School of Education at the university without serious loss of credit, and the recent conference arrangement between normal schools and university provides that students doing four years of standard work at a normal school may be admitted to graduate work in education at the university. The second group should be dealt with drastically, as the institution values its professional integrity. If elementary and high school instruction in this country is ever to be cleared of its traditionally random and trivial reputation, training agencies must insist on a curriculum so specific in character as to make its choice a fateful step in an individual's career. There will doubtless always be quondam teachers who fail and practise law, just as there are quondam physicians who fail and sell insurance, but it is intolerable for an honest training school so to relax its administration and enfeeble its courses as to put the transient at ease. Every normal school student should feel behind him a full tide of pressure from every quarter urging him to teach and to do nothing else, and he should contribute the impetus of his own clear decision to the general impulse.

UNITY OF AIM INCREASING

Finally, in the professional training itself there are discernible strong tendencies making for unity. The present schism in staff and curriculum was the result, at first, of the difficulty of securing competent teachers of academic subjects who possessed likewise a thorough training in education and successful experience in teaching children and youth. This is still an unusual combination, but, thanks to rapid growth of schools of education and to improved product in the normal schools, it is becoming less rare. In the case of the curriculum, the result seems to have been due partly to unsympathetic instructors, but more largely to a desire on all sides to swing as far as possible toward the collegiate idea and away from the earlier attitude. It is now evident that this emphasis has been greatly overdone. The normal school that is true to itself finds it impossible to be a college. A genuine professional purpose makes itself felt much further than the purely technical subjects; it governs the selection of material for every curriculum, it grips every course that is offered, and that in no perfunctory fashion as formerly, but with a clear, scientific conception of the ultimate aim in view. "With a mission like this, why waste time trying to be a college?" is the convincing retort of the modern training school. Again, if this clearer definition of aim affects the attendance of men at the schools, let the situation be faced frankly. There is nothing to be gained for the profession of teaching by catering to a set of individuals who definitely intend to make their normal school course and a year's teaching a step to other work. Such a procedure cheapens the course for its proper candidates, and advertises most effectually that teaching is a makeshift occupation and preparation therefor a farce. It is certainly most desirable to make the teaching profession attractive to men; but, given higher financial rewards, the surest way to convince them that there is something to it is to make it genuinely selective in respect to length and character of preparation. If they cannot be held on these terms, there is no help for it; any other condition is illusory and dishonest.

A NORMAL SCHOOL'S OBLIGATION TO THE STATE

The efficient teacher-training school of any grade is not to be measured by college, university, law, medical, or other liberal or professional institutions. These operate indirectly for the general good, but their direct aim is rather the intellectual or vocational benefit of the individual. The school for teachers, on the other hand, is the immediate instrument of the state for providing a given number and quality of public servants to discharge the main collective obligation of society to the next generation. Salaried staffs of physicians or lawyers supported by state or city for the whole people would imply a similar function in medical and law schools. Even so, the large number of teachers required, in proportion to the number of doctors and lawyers, would tend to elaborate and standardize the teacher-training agencies above other schools, Private and outside sources would not play so large a part, nor would such wide individual variation be acceptable in preparing five thousand as in furnishing three hundred.

In view of this peculiar relation to the state it is evident that, to be effective, the training institution should have two characteristics in a preëminent degree. First, it should have a vivid purpose. Its sole aim being to train teachers, every item of its organization should contribute either to the final excellence of its product, or to the creation and maintenance of conditions in its region that will make its product most successful. Irrelevant work that can be done elsewhere should be discontinued as soon as possible; bogus or uncertain candidates should be rejected; diversions of aim, however attractive, should be avoided. The school should do one thing and do it mightily. In the second place, it should be wholly responsive. First and last it serves the state and not individuals; as an efficient instrument it must be sensitive to control. New types or altered numbers of teachers, fresh courses to be added, higher standards to be set,—all of these should find the training school prepared for continual and automatic readjustment. The informed and authorized directors of the state's educational policy—and the state should obviously have such directors—should not find themselves helpless because of institutional conservatism, opposition of alumni, or local entanglements. To ensure this, the school clearly should not be entrusted to an irresponsible head for personal exploitation; the measure of excellence in administration should be a quiet and rapid accommodation to the changing demands of the state's educational authority. The loyalty of alumni should be won, not for persons or places, but for the skill with which the school does its work and for its flexible adaptation to its duties; the head of an institution who, by personal appeal to numerous or powerful graduates, seeks to swing his own policy at all costs is abusing his trust. Finally, to be responsive, the school must be free from local pressure and interference. The state as a whole invariably wants for itself better things, and defines those wants more wisely than can be the case in any but highly developed urban districts. To tie a school down to the limited vision of a small area is to deprive the community of that margin of superiority which the whole state has achieved and formulated.

9. James Earl Russell: "A Summary of Some of the Difficulties Connected with the Making of a Teachers College"*
(1924)

From 1897 to 1927, James Earl Russell was dean of Columbia University's Teachers College. His institution was peerless in national influence during those three decades. There were, of course, other distinguished graduate schools of education, but none approached Teachers College with respect to the number of students it trained for advanced degrees, the number of its graduates who assumed leadership as public school administrators or professors of education, or the geographical area over which its graduates moved. Though there were those who considered unsound the doctrines spread from Teachers College, no one could deny that these doctrines took wing.

Those to whom Russell referred in this essay as the "academically-minded" professors made of Teachers College a center of advanced research; those whom he called the "professionally-minded" kept it in close touch with practically oriented people in the elementary and

---

* American Association of Teachers Colleges, *Year Book, 1924*, pp. 23–28.

secondary schools. Teachers College was conflict-ridden, despite the fact that many of its critics erroneously described it as a temple dedicated to a single system of educational thought; and Russell barely got along "without bloodshed," not by luck, but by administrative skill. To keep the "academic" and "professional" interests balanced was hard enough in an independent graduate school of education such as Teachers College; it was even more difficult in multi-purpose colleges and universities, where both undergraduate and graduate departments of education were becoming tied more closely to the academic departments. Russell, it will be noted, called not for reconciliation; he promised only "constant conflict," hopefully mitigated by mutual understanding. Yet it may well be that the dichotomy seen by Russell was false, and that by perceiving "professionally" oriented people as nonacademic he encouraged them to be so, to the detriment of American education.

What I have in mind is not to tell anyone how to make a teachers college, but rather what are some of the difficulties in the making of one. I feel quite competent to speak on this larger topic. Each one, I dare say, has encountered difficulties, and they vary with the conditions under which we work.

A professional school of any kind, so far as I have observed, has to deal not only with professional studies, but with academic work as well. At the same time it is true that there are few so-called academic institutions in this country that are not in part professional or vocational schools. The moment a college permits differentiation by choice of subject or choice of curricula, that moment we are dealing with professional subjects, preprofessional at least, and there is no college that I know of that does not permit that differentiation.

Consider, then, the connotation of the terms "academic" and "professional." I mean by "academic" that type of work which leads the student to a constantly expanding knowledge of the subject. It is scientific, logical, all-inclusive. Such work well done gives breadth to life and universality of interests. The work of the world, however, demands concentration of powers and of interests on a particular job. This centering or narrowing upon a particular task is the chief characteristic of professional training. It does not follow, however, that subjects as taught in a professional school or an academic institution are perforce respectively either "academic" or "professional." The distinction comes not from the subject taught, but from the teaching of it. The fundamental fact is that teachers are either academically or professionally minded. Apparently we are born either pedagogical blonds or brunettes, or, as would be said in England, either little conservatives or little liberals. Perhaps it were better to say that each one of us is inclined towards one or the other of these extremes. Certainly there are all degrees of prejudice and bias directed one way or the other. The chief distinction lies in the difference of attitude taken by the teacher towards the student and the subject taught. The academically-minded teacher asks what the subject will do for the student; the professionally-minded teacher asks what the student will do with the subject.

Any subject may be given either an academic or a professional turn. Take physiology, for example. The academic treatment will regard the subject in its systematic development quite apart from its applications to any particular use. The vocational treatment calls for the selection of topics and materials that bear on the needs of practitioners—physicians, nurses, dentists, teachers—in short, anyone who has need of information that the subject can convey. The varying needs of various practitioners will be met by the selection of topics and the evaluation of materials in terms of the specific job. The teacher who is academically minded will make of it an academic subject, and the teacher who is professionally minded, will make it a professional or preprofessional subject. There is no subject that I know of which can not be taught academically or professionally.

I have to cite to you the experience most of us have had with the subject History of Education. Twenty-five years ago there was very little material assembled in this particular field. By research, materials were fitted into the subject called History of Education, and everything that came to that mill was grist for the teachers of education. The subject expanded and became larger and larger, until finally in the minds of most institutions the question arose as to whether it was of any particular value, because as an academic subject it was not fulfilling professional needs.[1]

I may go further, I think, and say that there is hardly a subject taught in our professional schools which may not be treated academically, or that certainly is not in danger of becoming an academic subject. With so much material so enthusiastically compiled in many fields, it is not surprising that some teachers become so enamored of their subject, that they cease to use it as a means of equipping their students for a particular task. Even practice

[1] Cf. Bernard Bailyn, *Education in the Forming of American Society* (Chapel Hill, N. C.: University of North Carolina Press, 1960), pp. 5-15. Bailyn suggests that the history of education has, in fact, been so dominated by the "professional view," in Russell's terms, that it has lost contact with "academic" history.—M. L. B.

teaching may be and is in some institutions an academic subject. But how can this be? Only when means are confounded with ends—when the elaboration of a system supplants the acquisition of technical skill as the end in view. Everything depends upon the mental set of the person doing the teaching.

I do not want you to get the impression from what I have said that I don't believe in academic work. The teacher who is absorbed in a subject, who believes in that subject, and who is willing to study it deeper and deeper, is a blessing to any school, and an inspiration to any class. More than one of us, in looking back over his own training, can recall teachers who, knowing and loving their subjects, taught us to know, love and enjoy them, not only for the time being, but for all time. How few such teachers there are! I can name only three in all my school days. I hope most of you can number more. We need many more such teachers, and anything a teacher-training school can do to bring out the love for a subject or ability to command a subject, is a part of our obligation. Moreover, academic training is the foundation upon which all professional training rests. Presumably also some part of this love of subject goes over into the work of the professional school for its enrichment and scholarly advancement.

I want to look at some of these problems from the administrative standpoint. We all have teachers in our professional schools either academically or professionally minded. What happens from the academic standpoint? The academically-minded teacher, believing firmly in the value of his subject in making the individual—and I do not want a teacher on my staff teaching a subject, who does not believe with all his soul in the efficacy of that subject—cannot help building up a department. At first he may be alone and do all the teaching. The time comes with the growth of the student body, when more help is needed. The old teacher then looks for a young instructor to help him. He goes to the president and says that he has two freshman classes he cannot teach, and asks for an assistant professor. But the college cannot afford an assistant professor. Time and again I have seen the demand drop from assistant professor at $3,000 to an assistant at $500. What happens? The newcomer is interested in a special phase of the subject, and because he is young, vigorous and in touch with the student body, he gathers a few novices under his wing. He teaches the freshmen on the side because he must do so to hold his job. This goes on for another year or two. The young man is interesting. He gathers in more and more followers in his specialty. Meantime, more freshmen come, until it is necessary to call in another assistant, and the process is repeated. This is what has been going on in our American colleges for the last thirty-five years. Departments have become stronger and stronger, and more and more courses are developed, until most colleges have been brought to the verge of bankruptcy, all because teachers have so loved their subjects that the purpose of the college has been forgotten or conveniently misplaced.

I want to tell you that this is one of the biggest problems we have to deal with today. It is just as apparent in the fields called Elementary or Rural Education, or Educational Administration, as it is in English or history. With the constant tendency to expand subjects academically, departments are the natural outgrowth of academic interest. I won't say that they don't have a place in academic institutions, because these are engaged in the business of expanding the world's horizon to meet the needs of a world at work. It does not follow, however, that there is a place in a professional school for departments. A professional school should have a faculty. A faculty exists for the direction of a homogeneous group of students toward some particular goal. The history of higher education shows that whenever a homogeneous group of students asks for guidance, a new faculty comes into existence. And in a faculty, it is obvious that the needs of such students can be met only by harmonious action. Departmental rivalry must give way to united effort. There is no more serious difficulty in the administration of a teacher-training institution than that growing out of the conflict between teachers who strive for the development of departments on one hand and those who emphasize the needs of the student body on the other.

It is from this source that spring most of the difficulties that we have to contend with in our higher institutions. You who have had experience with teacher training in university systems know what it means to be looked down upon by your academic brethren. The finger of scorn is pointed at you, they say your work is superficial, you are not scholarly, etc. All sorts of stinging terms are applied. On the other hand, the professionally minded are not loth to strike back. They call the others mossbacks, conservatives, antiques. We have here a psychological situation to be reckoned with. It cannot be dispelled by command or ridiculed out of existence.

There is not only this constant friction between the professionally and the academically minded, due to the tendency of the one to build up water-tight compartments and of the other to stress the work of the faculty as a whole, but it crops out in almost every undertaking. Take curricula making, for example. The academic staff will say that teachers are not fitted to teach after only two years of training; that they don't know their subjects well enough; hence the need of more years in the curriculum. But from the professional standpoint, there is only one way to determine the proper length of the curriculum. The limitation is the economic return that may be expected from professional service. I do not mean merely dollars and cents. There are certain economic returns in our profession that are more valuable than money. But by and large, those schools that overstep that particular boundary set by economic conditions are in danger of getting the dubs in their classes at the expense of turning away the brightest candidates. Those below par mentally or personally will stick out a longer set program, simply because they must get every advantage possible for the competition of later professional life. There is nothing surer, in my judgment, than if you overreach yourself in length of curricula, other things being equal, your brightest students will tend to go to other institutions or into other professions, while the poorest you will always have with you. Our duty to the community at large, our obligation to the profession, demand that we shall keep up as near the top limit as possible, but self preservation demands that we do not overstep the line. This is a difficult administration problem to meet.

I have already referred to those subjects which we think of as professional, but which, in the hands of some professors, become out-and-out academic. A few years ago in making a survey of my institution I found that so-called Educational Administration had been so elaborated into courses that it needed four or five catalogue pages to list them. It was obvious that no prospective school superintendent with only one year at his disposal could possibly take all of them, or even enough to fit him for his job. The outcome is that we have shifted not only the type of course, but the designation of these departments as well. We are no longer listing them under Educational Administration as formerly, but are using the caption "Courses for Superintendents," "Courses for High School Principals," "Courses for Supervisors," etc. Just that change in phraseology is indicative of a radical change in content and method which required some years of effort to bring to light. Not how much do you know and how much can you give in your course, but what does your student need, and how much can he afford to take, and how long can he afford to stay to get the things he needs, are the questions which determine whether our courses are academic or professional. This means that the academic red tape of hour-week-term courses goes by the board. There is no excuse for padding a professional course to make it fit into an academic schedule.

I want to say this in conclusion—there is abundant ground for compromise in every professional school. We want some academically-minded teachers, because some subjects should be taught academically. The curricula, however, must be judged by professional standards, and some courses must be given in a professional manner for professional ends. The academically-minded teacher will stand on what he calls the scholarly basis, and we want it because it is much needed. The professionally-minded teacher will stand just as vigorously for the professional evaluation of those subjects to meet the needs of professional students. The two will be constantly combatting each other, and that administrative official is lucky who can get on without bloodshed. This, then, is the one thing to do, in my judgment—I believe that it is possible to have these two groups understand each other. I believe it is possible to convince the professionally-minded of the need for scholarly work by academic teachers. And on the other hand, I believe that it is possible to bring the academically minded to a realization that they are working in a professional school, and that at some stage they must shift from the logical order of presentation over to the professional attitude. When we can get them to call each other friends, and even to admire each other for what each gives, then the millenium has almost arrived. Those institutions which are able to bring the two types together and say, "Together we are working for the best interests of our students and of the institution, as well as for the best interest of scholarship," are indeed fortunate.

10. George S. Counts: "Break the Teacher Training Lockstep"* (1935)

The Social Frontier *originated during one of the rare periods of rapprochement between professors of the social sciences and professors of education. Its board of contributors included John Dewey, Merle Curti, Broadus Mitchell, Charles A. Beard, Lewis Mumford, Henry P. Fairchild, Joseph K. Hart, Boyd H. Bode, and George A. Coe; its editor was George S. Counts, who may yet prove to have been America's most insightful early student of the relationship between the schools and social interest groups. The magazine emerged amid screaming protest against the conditions that had created the Great Depression. It died shortly thereafter, when vigorous protest went out of style as the approach of World War II brought a unifying factor to American life and prosperity to the American economy. The movement represented by* The Social Frontier *also produced several volumes for the American Historical Association's Commission on the Social Studies and a number of seminal books by professional educators. Examples of the former are Howard K. Beale's two volumes on freedom of teachers and Merle Curti's* The Social Ideas of American Educators; *of the latter, perhaps* The Educational Frontier, *edited by William Heard Kilpatrick, is most representative.*

* *The Social Frontier,* I (June, 1935), 6–7.

In the present era, one in which The Education of American Teachers *by the conservative James Bryant Conant has rocked the education establishment with charges that it is excessively rigid, overly committed to standardization, and not as imaginative as it could be, one is fascinated to read the same criticisms leveled a generation ago by men on the democratic left. The Social Frontiersmen were temperamentally rebellious; Conant is not. Can it be that the tendencies that blocked the aspirations of radicals thirty years ago have become so exaggerated that now even the moderate is frustrated?*

From state to state over the entire land the curricula of the public normal schools and teachers colleges are as like as peas in a pod. Only with extreme rarity does a state or city educational administrator display real statesmanship by looking the teacher training problem in the face and proposing a program at variance with tradition. So-called reforms there have been; they pass in waves from region to region—patchwork tinkerings with the familiar curricular pattern. The American Association of Teachers Colleges appears to be using its newly attained prestige to put the final stamp of approval upon well-established and vested methods of preparing teachers for the public schools. Various "standardizing" agencies are hard at work ironing out the few remaining sectional variations in policy and technique among professional schools of education.

The most radical thing that has happened in recent years in this field has been the practically universal extension of the training period for elementary school teachers from two years to three or four years beyond the high school. This time extension, which has considerably increased state educational expenditures in a period of economic stress, obviously cannot be depended upon markedly to raise the qualitative level of teaching. It has, however, been hailed by many educators as the final answer to all the criticisms levelled at the inadequacy of the teaching in American public schools. The strenuous agitation to have every public school teacher bear a degree after her name exemplifies a common tendency among educators to prefer appearance to reality. It was easily assumed that the main fault with the traditional teacher training program was its briefness. Thus the cause for the reported poor quality of teaching was shifted from the *nature* of the training which candidates received to the *shortness* of the training period. The remedy which naturally enough suggested itself was more years of the same kind of training. An examination of the recently revised courses of study in the state teachers colleges shows quite clearly that the new ones are mere padded versions of the old.

Rapid advance in the social sciences together with the remarkable changes wrought in the professional education of young men and women for medical, engineering, and law careers renders demonstrably false any belief that the education of teachers now approaches a stage of perfection. Standardization of practice, no matter how worthy in conception, has no place in a field which seems so obviously to have reached only the early stages of experimentation.

What a setting for experimental teacher training programs our state-controlled public school systems provide! State educational leaders with vision should glory in the experimenter's paradise which is theirs. Many different types of state teacher training programs are imaginable. The possibilities for determining the major outlines of a stable American policy in the professional education of teachers are illimitable, if only vision and daring combine to replace outworn practices. Already the private and semi-public universities are experimenting with fresh programs of teacher preparation and the fundamental background for intelligently guided departures from tradition has been explored. Some of the major variables in teacher training are well known. Others will be discovered. But as yet even the willingness to vary factors like selective admissions, the curriculum, and the utilization of master teachers, has been lacking.

Constructive efforts to set up adequate selective machinery for candidates have been instituted in most training centers, public and private. But only the surface of this problem has been scratched. A few of the utterly unlikely candidates are being eliminated. The real need is to construct selective machinery in terms solely of the high cultural quality and professional aptness desired in the young men and women to whom the basic education of American boys and girls is to be entrusted. The present over-supply of so-called trained teachers is a golden opportunity to cut the number of young people entering teacher training institutions to a relatively drastic minimum. Psychological science, personnel service, the experience of other professions upon this problem cry out to be applied.

The familiar curricular pattern of orientation courses, subject matter courses, theory courses, observation courses, and practice-teaching assignments is but a conglomeration of precepts and practices inherited from the more limited environment of a former day. No matter how much science in the way of statistical summaries, surveys by experts, and correlational studies is applied to this type of curriculum, the best result obtainable can be only a minor refinement added to something fundamentally inadequate. It is necessary to get completely outside the present teacher training picture and from a new vantage point to consider modern educational needs and modern teaching opportunities. The buildings and grounds now available can be used as well for new techniques, new purposes, new attitudes, as for old. It is conceivable for instance that if the selection of trainees be properly made, the advanced academic education provided for prospective teachers can consist entirely of cultural material, especially selected and communicated, to promote mellow wisdom, imaginative vision, and a driving educative zeal—qualities sadly lacking in the average school teacher today. It is also possible that the theoretic professional background so necessary in the teaching art may be provided in the highest degree by a carefully planned and extended interneship service under master teachers in particular studies or at particular educational levels.

Perhaps the most neglected opportunity in the field today is the universal failure to make use of those teachers now practicing in the public schools who have proved highly capable in stimulating the learning powers of pupils. These artists of the profession exercise almost no influence upon teacher training at present. An appalling waste is involved in thus denying to apprentices constant intimate give and take with masters. It may be said with impunity that until master teachers are placed in a key position in teacher training programs, no real progress in raising qualitative standards in the profession will be recorded.

Those of us who are interested in making the educational profession function adequately in realizing a new American society equal to modern economic and cultural opportunities, must appreciate the necessity for breaking the present lockstep in teacher training. It will be necessary boldly to establish experimental procedures of far-reaching scope in different states as a means to reliable, efficient, and stable programs for attaining broad professional objectives. The stakes are a teaching profession capable of weighting public opinion in the direction of increased reliance upon experimental intelligence.

11. Commission on Teacher Education: *The Improvement of Teacher Education** (1946)

In 1938, the American Council on Education's Commission on Teacher Education undertook a massive project, which involved experimental action in twenty institutions of higher education and fourteen public school systems. The enterprise cannot be characterized accurately as scientific experimentation; the reports, twenty-seven publications in all, tended to be largely descriptive of activities or points of view. The commission came increasingly to direct its efforts toward the discovery of processes that would expedite reform and increase co-operation among the agencies involved in teacher education. Its final recommendations asserted explicitly that the search for universal formulae is foolish. Nevertheless, the commission did set forth general guidelines, some of which are reproduced below.

The commission was chaired by Edward S. Evenden of Teachers College, Columbia University, who had earlier headed a teacher education study under the sponsorship of the United States Office of Education.† The director

* *The Improvement of Teacher Education: A Final Report by the Commission on Teacher Education* (Washington, D.C.: American Council on Education, 1946), pp. 82–102.

† The survey (1927–1933) was the second of the massive studies of American teacher education undertaken during the first half of the twentieth century. (The first was the Missouri study [see Chap-

of the project was Karl Bigelow, a Harvard-trained economist who became professor of education at Teachers College; and his central staff included, among others, W. Earl Armstrong, who, as executive officer of the National Commission on Accreditation for Teacher Education, became a dominant figure in American teacher education.

GENERAL EDUCATION

The Commission does not consider that its experience, within and beyond the cooperative study, equips it to speak with authority regarding all of the issues connected with the matter of general education. It believes that many of these must for some time continue to be the subject of debate among educators and that such debate should be encouraged, especially among members of the same faculty. There is no doubt that dissatisfaction with the present chaotic situation with respect to general education is powerful and widespread. Conflicting educational philosophies and the usual preoccupation of individual faculty members with responsibilities that are not general—with, for example, their own departmental specialties—make agreement difficult. At the same time, however, interest in the achievement of greater unity is

---

ter 10]; the American Council study discussed here was the third.) The survey of the United States Office of Education was the most comprehensive of the lot with respect to the amount of factual information it assembled. By 1933, when Evenden prepared his *Summary and Interpretation*, it was possible to know more fully than at any previous time in our history what was actually happening in teacher education. To the claim that an extract from this volume should have been reproduced here, I plead "no contest"; the decision to exclude it was an arbitrary one. See United States Office of Education, *National Survey of the Education of Teachers*, Bulletin 1933, No. 10, Vol. VI.

insistent, as is the desire to make general education more vitally concerned with the related needs of man and society.

The Commission's own judgments respecting the general education of teachers may be summarized as follows:

1. Teachers should receive the best possible general education, not only in order that they may share in what ought to be the birthright of all young Americans today, but also because to them is entrusted considerable responsibility for the general education of all young Americans tomorrow.

2. The aim of general education should be to enable young men and women to meet effectively the most important and widespread problems of personal and social existence; in the case of prospective teachers such education should seek to further the development of knowledge, skills, attitudes, and interests that are fundamentally related to needs and responsibilities shared with contemporaries destined for other vocations.

3. While general education may be usefully contrasted with special or vocational education, it ought not, as conducted, to ignore the implications of the special or vocational purposes of students; nor should professional education be carried on wholly without reference to students' more general needs: an integration of general and professional education should be sought.

4. At least three-eighths of the college experience of a prospective teacher should have as its primary objectives those properly ascribable to general education.

5. While elements of general education may well predominate during the first two college years they should neither monopolize nor be limited to this period: some educational experiences related to vocational purposes should be provided as soon as the latter are formed; and

Commission on Teacher Education

the idea that general education may be considered as "completed" at some particular time should not be encouraged.

6. The contemporary trend toward balance and integration in general education is significant and deserves support. This implies a basic pattern of broad courses, each developed with the special purposes of general education in mind, each requiring a fairly substantial block of time, and all planned in relation to one another.

7. The trend toward the use of more in the way of nonverbal methods of instruction and student expression also deserves encouragement. Firsthand experience, as well as motion pictures and the radio, should supplement books as tools for learning, and students should be helped to express what they have learned not only in words but through the arts and social action.

8. General education should be concerned with the body and the emotions as well as with the intellect.

9. Students should be given a more active, responsible role in the planning and carrying out of their own general education. This implies that instruction should be flexibly administered to provide for responsiveness to individual differences.

10. A leading aim of college programs of general, or for that matter of professional, education should be to make it probable that graduates will continue their growth in understanding and competence after they have become teachers.

11. The development of superior programs of general education on particular campuses requires local group endeavor: faculty unity is prerequisite to curricular unity.

12. Such shared effort should be designed to reveal

and clarify existing differences of opinion, to increase general understanding of the needs of students and society, and to obtain open-minded consideration of educational thought and action as expressed and carried out elsewhere.

13. Helpful in facilitating improvements in general education have been faculty group discussions, special studies, interviews with students and alumni, community and service-area surveys, visits to schools and to other colleges, use of consultants, and participation in general education workshops.

14. Willingness to sanction the testing of new ideas respecting general education by experimental-minded staff members working with special groups of students has often helped to resolve differences of speculative opinion and led to an extension of sound reforms.

ADVANCED SUBJECT-MATTER PREPARATION

In several of the universities with which the Commission was associated special attempts were made to improve the advanced subject-matter preparation of teachers for the secondary schools.[1] These efforts were in each case carried on by committees representing both the schools or departments of education and the appropriate subject-matter faculties. The attacks were invariably made with reference to teachers for particular fields—for example,

[1] For further discussion bearing on this topic, see W. Earl Armstrong, Ernest V. Hollis, and Helen E. Davis, *The College and Teacher Education* (Washington: American Council on Education, 1944), Chapter IV and pp. 214–22, and American Council on Education, Commission on Teacher Education, *Teachers for Our Times* (Washington: American Council on Education, 1944), especially Chapters II and IV.

English, social studies, natural science, or vocational agriculture—but the general implications of recommendations were borne in mind. In most cases, indeed, the committees found themselves concerned with questions of general education before they were through.

These efforts were not unaccompanied with difficulties, and in most instances less progress in the way of reform was made during the course of the study than optimists in the several situations had hoped for; but the work done resulted in distinctly better mutual understanding, cleared a good deal of ground, brought some significant changes, and laid a substantial basis for further advance. The fact is, of course, that there is ordinarily such distance between educationists and subject-matter professors that it is inevitable that considerable time and energy must be expended before genuine agreement between them as to principles and desirable changes respecting teacher education can be expected. The work of the committees mentioned was successful in greatly increasing the area of such agreement.

It is the striking fact that each of the committees referred to undertook early in their work to study the schools to which their graduates went as teachers, and to receive testimony from such graduates as were in a position to discuss candidly both their preparatory and teaching experiences and the relations they saw between the two. This proved to be a very valuable procedure. It removed the focus of attention from the often apparently conflicting theories of the committee members and rooted discussion in realities the relevance of which all were ready to admit. The suggestions from the field, moreover, bore impartially on all aspects of the preparatory program so that the faculty representatives of no particular department were likely to be made to feel that they were the exclusive objects of criticism. Of course, the committees quite properly retained the right of exercising their critical judgments regarding what they discovered to be going on in the schools and what was urged upon them by the field. Not only did they consider it their final responsibility to decide how their institution might best undertake to meet revealed needs, but they also felt free to be critical of the demands placed upon teachers in some situations. The process was one of give and take.

Those who took vigorous part, through the course of a year or two, in the studies under consideration felt the experience to have been eminently worth while, developed significant new insights, and reached satisfying conclusions. They became convinced that closer collaboration between educationists and subject-matter experts was both possible and desirable in the preparation of teachers and that a broader preparation in fields to be taught, through the medium of instruction more definitely related to a teacher's problems, should be sought after. They proposed a variety of curricular reforms, which may, however, be treated together.

In two situations the designation or appointment of department members to take particular responsibility for matters of teacher preparation was recommended, in one case it being urged that such persons should become liaison professors sitting on both the arts and education faculties. Better integration of the prospective teacher's work in education and in subject-matter fields was declared to be important: in one university where courses in education had been ordinarily concentrated in a fifth, or first graduate, year this existing arrangement was roundly condemned. The committee, three-fourths of the members of which were not from the faculty of education, called it a fallacy to suppose "that training in education is something that can be applied from above at the end of another program; that it is training which in a fifth year can miraculously be clapped on top of a four-year bachelor of arts degree pursued without reference to the vocation of teaching."[2]

The committees became vividly aware of the fact that existing subject-matter courses and concentration requirements were often relatively unsuited to the needs of prospective teachers. They were planned and controlled by subject-matter specialists who tended to think departmentally, to see elementary courses as primarily preparatory for those in advance, to believe that only a relatively large amount of work in their field could provide a respectable knowledge thereof, and to be especially interested in providing preparation for graduate school specialization in their subjects. Prospective secondary school teachers, however, have to look forward to the probability of being required to teach several subjects and to handle them broadly: they need breadth and integration of preparation. An example of the difficulty that arises can be cited from the case of an institution where teachers of vocational agriculture are prepared. It was evident that they needed to learn something about the care of all kinds of farm creatures, but to do this they had to take an impossible number of separate courses each dealing with its own distinct animal or fowl. A not dissimilar situation faced students who wished to prepare for the teaching of general science.

The committees recognized that there were two courses

[2] The university in question was Harvard, which did not participate in any of the Commission's cooperative studies, but which carried out the investigation described with financial assistance obtained from the Commission. The quotation is from the Harvard committee's report, *The Training of Secondary School Teachers* (Cambridge: Harvard University Press, 1942), p. 124.

of action they might follow in attempting to deal with this general situation: they might urge the development and introduction of new courses particularly designed for prospective teachers or they might be satisfied to propose a new grouping of existing courses. Generally the first possibility appealed on logical grounds but was eventually, for practical reasons, not immediately recommended. Where favorable response to the idea could be anticipated it was pressed, but the committees usually concluded that the less radical step had better be proposed to begin with. Even as it was they ran into some difficulties: they often discovered that their colleagues, who had not had the advantage of their study experience, were resistant even to changes which the committee members felt were mild compared with what might sensibly have been suggested.

There were many reasons for such resistance. General conservatism and indifference or even hostility to teacher education played their roles, as did departmental loyalties and unreadiness to agree to reduction of requirements in one's own field. Faith in the virtues of emphatic specialization was an influential element in several situations, as was the related conviction that any needed leeway in the existing pattern could be far more wisely obtained by sacrifices made by the other fellow. In one instance where a divisional committee had ventured to recommend changes affecting the local pattern of requirements in the area of general education, the opposition of the departments that stood likely to lose students and status received support from others who felt that the traditions of a liberal education were being attacked.

But such a candid account of the difficulties that were encountered when efforts were made to reform the subject-matter preparation of teachers should not be permitted to leave an impression of frustration. Progress was made. The university whose committee recommended that courses in education and advanced courses in subject-matter be dovetailed through three years following completion of the sophomore program, and that arrangements be made for the closer and more continuous cooperation of educationists and subject-matter people in planning and supervising preparatory programs, saw these and related recommendations fully accepted by the faculty. This represented a by no means slight advance in this particular setting. Specific changes were also accomplished elsewhere, and setbacks that occurred were not regarded as necessarily permanent. But what is most important is that through earnest group study in which there was representative participation, and through the steady growth of understanding of the real problems of the schools and of the teachers therein, distinct advances were made in the achievement of mutual understanding and in the laying of a reliable foundation for further progress in future.

The Commission may now summarize some of its own general conclusions regarding the role of subject-matter instruction, over and above that which may be considered as falling within the area of general education, in the preparation of a teacher:

1. There can be no doubt that a high degree of scholarly competence is essential in a teacher; such competence requires not only knowledge and personal skill but also the ability to use both effectively in the teaching relationship.

2. It is essential that subject-matter instructors whose students are preparing to teach should be sympathetic to their purpose and informed as to the problems they will face when they enter upon their professional careers.

3. It is also important that such instructors should

work more closely and realistically with representatives of schools and departments of education in identifying the needs of prospective teachers and planning curricula in which both subject-matter and professional elements will be functionally combined.

4. The familiar major-minor pattern of subject-matter preparation is being desirably paralleled in many colleges by arrangements that provide for more integration and greater attention to bearings on personal and social needs. For example, divisional as contrasted with departmental majors are increasingly available to undergraduates. Such arrangements offer particular advantages to students who are preparing to teach in modern elementary and secondary schools.

PROFESSIONAL EDUCATION: GENERAL

There were, of course, numerous attacks made on problems related to the more strictly professional education of teachers in the course of the cooperative study.[3] Some of these were in relation to other efforts: all of the university committees discussed in the preceding section got more or less deeply into a consideration of professional instruction. Some dealt generally with the professional part of the program and some with particular aspects.

There were two subjects of study that received outstanding attention as essential elements in the preparation of all teachers: individual human beings—particularly children; and human beings organized in the mass

[3] For further discussion bearing on this general topic, see *The College and Teacher Education*, Chapters V, VI, and VIII; Charles E. Prall, *State Programs for the Improvement of Teacher Education* (Washington: American Council on Education, 1946), Part Three; Maurice E. Troyer and C. Robert Pace, *Evaluation in Teacher Education* (Washington: American Council on Education, 1944), Chapters V and VI; and *Teachers for Our Times*, especially Chapters III and IV.

—particularly the community. It was, in other words, generally agreed that teachers need a special understanding of the young persons with whom they work and also of the society for and in which they work. While these were seen as professional requirements it was also recognized that in part, at least, personal and social understanding had reasonable claims to being considered elements in general education. It is not surprising, therefore, that courses designed to promote these kinds of understanding were variously classified in different institutions.

CHILD GROWTH AND DEVELOPMENT

Of course, the study of human nature, through courses in general and in educational psychology, has long been considered an indispensable part of the preparation of teachers, but the tendency observable in the cooperative study—partly, certainly, because of the influence of the Commission's leadership—was to substitute a different type of approach.[4] This was characterized by an effort to

[4] For an extended treatment of this topic, see American Council on Education, Staff of the Division on Child Development and Teacher Personnel, Commission on Teacher Education, *Helping Teachers Understand Children* (Washington: American Council on Education, 1945). This volume describes in detail a three-year study program carried on by experienced teachers, but its implications for teacher preparation are extensive and clear. More explicitly relating to teacher education is a report of a special committee of the American Association of Teachers Colleges made at the conclusion of a year's work at the collaboration center at the University of Chicago: *Child Growth and Development Emphases in Teacher Education* (Oneonta, N. Y.: American Association of Teachers Colleges, 1944). See further the bibliography in the appendix to this report of mimeographed material produced at the collaboration center. Also, *The College and Teacher Education,* Chapters V and VI *passim; State Programs for the Improvement of Teacher Education,* Chapter VII; *Evaluation in Teacher Education,* pp. 137–42; and *Teachers for Our Times,* pp. 92–126 and 165–68.

draw on a variety of disciplines—the psychological, biological, and sociological—in order to provide a picture of human beings as both whole and growing organisms, responding both to internal drives and external influences. It was also usual to balance the study of scientific generalizations about human development and behavior with practice in the gathering and organization of facts respecting actual individual children and covering a considerable period of time. The aim was to develop ability to use the generalizations in interpreting particular cases and formulating plans for dealing with them wisely. The Commission believes that the superior values of these methods of preparing teachers to understand the human organism with which they are to work have been clearly demonstrated.

SOCIAL UNDERSTANDING

The Commission is equally impressed by the importance of efforts to develop social and community understanding in teachers.[5] A teacher's behavior should be guided not only by a grasp of the needs and capacities for response of his pupils, but also by an informed awareness of the needs and expectations of the culture of which the school is an expression. Knowledge of the immediate community is important. This will increase the teacher's understanding of the children and their opportunities,

---

[5] For additional material bearing on this topic, see Gordon W. Blackwell, *Toward Community Understanding* (Washington: American Council on Education, 1943); *The College and Teacher Education*, Chapters III, V, and VI *passim; State Programs for the Improvement of Teacher Education*, Chapters III, IV, and V *passim; Evaluation in Teacher Education*, pp. 142–45 and 203–18; and *Teachers for Our Times*, Chapter II and pp. 139–41, 158–59, and 168–71.

will sensitize him to local problems and resources, will help him to perform his professional role effectively.

The good teacher will know how to adjust his behavior sensitively to a particular school situation, taking intelligent account, for example, of the differences between an urban and a rural environment, or a homogeneous upperclass community and one marked by tensions related to poverty, and to differences of nationality, race, and religion. Such considerations have evident implications for the preparation of teachers. Not only should they learn the importance of community understanding for their profession but they should be taught how to develop it. They should learn, through practice as well as precept, how to study a community and how to make use of what is learned in developing teaching procedures. Nor should the preparatory experience fail to impress prospective teachers with a sense of obligation, personal as well as professional, to take a responsible part in community affairs. Again, the how as well as the why should be taught, and experience as well as classroom instruction provided.

Of course, the focus of attention should not be limited to the immediate community. In teachers, more than in most other classes of citizens, it is important that there should reside a considerable understanding of their region, their country, and their world. As has been emphasized, a teacher's broad social responsibility is fundamental. He can scarcely discharge it wisely in ignorance of American and other cultures. The implications for preparatory programs are clear.

In the cooperative study various means were employed to develop in prospective teachers such elements of community and social understanding as have been stressed. In some situations special courses were created, in others elements of social and community study were included in professional core units, and in both of these cases direct community contacts, preceding as well as in connection with student teaching, were often provided. The goals differed: general understanding of the values, structure, and functioning of society—especially our own—skill in community analysis and evaluation, ability to adapt oneself to a new community environment, skill in discerning community resources and in utilizing them for educational ends, and predisposition to enter responsibly into community affairs.

The Commission considers that continued effort along such lines is essential to the improvement of teacher education. It believes that reading and discussion should be strongly supplemented by firsthand experience—by opportunities to observe community and broader social realities directly and under skilled guidance, to practice techniques of social inquiry, and to participate responsibly in community life. Contacts should be made with social-service agencies, with libraries and museums, and with neighborhoods and homes. Travel should be encouraged. With proper advice and guidance many prospective teachers can make rich educational use of vacation periods for the extension of social understanding, even—and perhaps particularly—in connection with earning opportunities. Such guidance should be provided.

CREATIVE EXPRESSION

A further element that the Commission considers important in the preparation of teachers (though it cannot claim that it was widely emphasized in the colleges participating in the cooperative study) is education in the expressive arts.[6] It would be possible to urge the value of this as a part of general as well as of professional education. The case for the arts in teacher education rests, indeed, on both foundations. First of all, artistic activity offers a unique means of emotional release and creative expression that is particularly valuable to personality in our tense and mechanical times. Then such activity, because it does not call for the use of words and is a matter of putting parts together with emphasis on the emotional content and effectiveness of the whole, provides a greatly needed balance to the intellectual, verbal, and analytical elements of experience with which teaching is ordinarily so predominantly concerned. Furthermore, acquaintance with the arts and some even minor skill in artistic expression help a teacher to enrich instruction in many ways and to understand and establish communication with children who are more responsive to other than verbal symbols. Finally, an appreciation of the arts is certainly to be considered a characteristic of any well educated person.

DIRECT EXPERIENCE

The reader will have observed the suggestion in the discussions of child study, social study, and art activity—all

---

[6] See in connection with this topic, Ray N. Faulkner and Helen E. Davis, *Teachers Enjoy the Arts* (Washington: The American Council on Education, 1943). This is a report on art experiences had by teachers who were attending workshops, but it possesses definite implications for teacher preparation. See also *The College and Teacher Education*, pp. 174–77, and *Teachers for Our Times*, pp. 77–81 and 137–38.

three—that direct experience should be included.[7] Children and communities should be studied, not merely studied about, and actual artistic creation, however amateur, should be attempted. Such attempts at the mingling of theoretical inquiry with active contacts with reality were markedly displayed in the cooperative study. Prospective teachers were enabled to begin observation of children relatively early in their preparatory careers, and opportunities were provided whereby they might work with young people responsibly and under guidance in varied school and other situations. They were also led to study communities at first hand and to take part in their affairs. Such direct experiences were designed to serve a number of purposes: to extend the basis upon which students and their advisers could check the wisdom of tentative vocational choices; to enable the students to comprehend and judge better for themselves the theoretical formulations that were being presented in class; to sensitize them to the uniqueness of individual human beings and communities and help them to guard against using mechanically generalizations regarding either; and to develop in them feelings of ease, security, and competence in real situations.

Direct experience was arranged for in a variety of ways. Laboratory schools, art studios, and student organizations provided readily accessible opportunities on the campus. Relationships were also established with nearby public and private schools, with social agencies of various kinds, and with other institutions in the immediate or more extended community. These relationships were

[7] For additional material bearing on this topic, see *The College and Teacher Education*, pp. 174–79 and 304–5, and *Teachers for Our Times*, pp. 135–37, and *Toward Community Understanding, passim;* also the reference relating to student teaching, pp. 100–1 of the present report.

of such sort that advantages accrued to outside bodies as well as to the prospective teachers and the college programs. A number of colleges and universities undertook systematically to help students to use their vacation periods in ways calculated to contribute definitely to their well rounded development as teachers. Counselorship in summer camps made possible growth in the understanding of children. Jobs in trade or industry or on the farm enabled prospective teachers to increase their grasp of the nature of important aspects of American life. Travel provided opportunities for the expansion of horizons and the reduction of provincialism. One university arranged for most of its sophomores to spend the three-week period before the beginning of college classes in the fall giving full-time service to various public schools scattered through the state that it served. Many of the activities listed had always been available to undergraduates during vacation periods, but the deliberate effort of college faculties to see to it that their educational possibilities were well realized represented a relatively new and a very important development.

LARGER INSTRUCTIONAL UNITS

One marked trend in the cooperative study was in the direction of combining the elements of professional education into a few relatively large and inclusive units; there was a distinct movement away from reliance upon a great number of short, specialized, and quite distinct courses.[8] The purpose was to assure greater continuity of experience and closer attention to interrelationships of

[8] For further treatment of this topic, see *The College and Teacher Education,* Chapters V and VI *passim,* and *State Programs for the Improvement of Teacher Education,* Chapter IX.

various kinds, and at the same time to make possible more flexibility and variety. The development was closely tied up, it should be added, with the tendency to provide for more direct experience, which was, indeed, facilitated by the arrangement in large blocks of time.

At one university where two undergraduate colleges were cooperating with the graduate school of education in conducting an experimental three-year program, three-hour seminars in the junior and senior years were succeeded in the graduate year by a three-hour central seminar, a two-hour divisional seminar (in the humanities and language arts; the social sciences; science and mathematics; art and music; home and community life, health, and recreation; or elementary education), and three to four hours of student teaching. The work of these seminars—planned to constitute a unified but flexible whole, and supervised by committees of educationists and subject-matter specialists—combined the integrated organization of subject matter, curriculum planning, teaching methods, and evaluation. Continuous guidance was also a function assigned to seminar leaders. A close relationship was maintained with the work of student teaching.

STUDENT PARTICIPATION

One important advantage—and indeed one definite purpose—of the large blocks of time arrangement in professional education was the opportunity provided for more participation by the prospective teachers themselves in planning the details of the educational experiences enjoyed.[9] As a matter of fact the idea that students

[9] For further treatment of this topic, see *The College and Teacher Education,* Chapters II, III, V, and VI *passim* and pp. 302-4, and *Evaluation in Teacher Education,* Chapters III–VI *passim* and pp. 4, 14-15, and 364-65.

should be worked with, rather than on, affected college practice in many ways. In student personnel programs, as was previously noted, the aim increasingly was to encourage personal responsibility by helping the individual to estimate his own strengths and weaknesses and reach his own judgments as to what he must undertake to do in order to attain an adequate level of professional competence. In programs of general education as well faculty members found it advantageous to arrange for undergraduates to share in planning and evaluating details of the course of instruction. The same was true of professional courses, even when not consolidated, and of student teaching. The participation occurred not only in connection with particular courses or other types of educational experience, but sometimes on the higher level of institutional planning: there was, for example, experimentation with the inclusion of student representatives on faculty committees with large responsibilities and even in general faculty meetings.

There were several reasons for this very striking trend toward provision for more responsible participation by undergraduates in the determination of their educational programs. Basic was the desire to realize the implications of democratic theory. Belief in the worth and potentialities of the individual required that he should be not merely permitted but actually stimulated to share in choosing a course of action in the light of his personal goals. Conviction as to the importance of group methods, in which all give and take according to their several powers and needs, urged the employment of such methods in educational planning. Adherence to the idea that self-guidance according to the dictates of one's own reason should receive all possible encouragement further demanded that students be not relieved of the responsibility of choice.

All such considerations, it will be observed, are as applicable to college students who are not preparing to teach as to prospective teachers. They also have implications for the conduct of education in the secondary and elementary schools. While the manner and degree of student participation in educational planning will appropriately vary with age, experience, and other individual characteristics, provision for such participation cannot properly be neglected even in the earliest grades. Because this is true it follows that there is a special, professional reason for such provision in programs of teacher education. A teacher whose own education has been mostly a matter of passive acquiescence in programs and procedures predetermined by his instructors is not likely easily and effectively to lead his own pupils to share responsibility in the planning of their educational experiences. Prospective teachers particularly, therefore, should be treated as persons, as capable of participating intelligently in the determination of their own educational courses.

But it is not only because of the experience it provides in pupil-teacher planning that more student participation is professionally advantageous to prospective teachers. As it works out—or can be made to work out—in practice it brings the individual into closer and more significant contact with the whole process of institutional planning. The sense of what the faculty as a whole is driving at is heightened and the values of continuous cooperation in thought and action among staff members become evident. Thus the teacher-to-be begins to see how important it will be for him to take part in the affairs of his own school and system when he enters upon his professional work. And he begins to develop skill in democratic group work of the sort that it is desirable he should be able to help carry on at that time.

For all reasons given, the Commission strongly favors the trend toward increased student participation in programs of teacher education. It hopes that more and more will be attempted in this direction. From its experience, however, it offers two warnings. The first is that no efforts can succeed that are not genuine, that do not actually provide students with influence. Better an honest dictatorship than a false democracy. Students who are likely to make good teachers for our times will not long be deceived by merely being permitted now and then to hold the reins. Of course, they will make some mistakes if they are given real responsibility, but they can learn from such mistakes. And it is at least an open question whether the faculties might not have made even worse mistakes without them.

But in any case student participation does not imply at all that the faculty should not participate. One of the values of the process is the experience it brings in learning how to assess and accept the contributions to a group process of classes and individuals representing special resources and responsibilities. This brings us to the second warning. It is possible for faculties newly enthusiastic over the idea of student participation to ask more of undergraduates than their experience has prepared them to perform. The Commission observed a few examples of this sort which might easily have resulted in unjustifiable discouragement with the whole idea of student participation.

Both pitfalls mentioned are likely to be avoided when certain conditions are present. The process should be seen as a potentially significant means to larger and very important ends; then the temptation to employ it in dogged mechanical fashion, rather than with human artistry, will be avoided. An experimental temper should be preserved: results should be evaluated by students *and* faculty and procedures modified in the light of experience. Perhaps most important of all a relationship of mutual friendly confidence should be cultivated: genuine participation requires give and take which is really possible only where personal relationships have been established.

STUDENT TEACHING: RELATED ARRANGEMENTS

Trends with respect to student teaching in the cooperative study further exemplified the movement in the direction of program integration.[10] With increasing emphasis on direct experience, moreover, not only did the character of arrangements for student teaching tend to be affected, but these also came to be viewed as culminating rather than as standing more or less alone. There was a marked tendency to provide for considerable precedent experience with children in school and other situations.

The colleges equipped with campus schools were particularly well situated to enable students to observe children and participate in their guidance in connection with various courses beginning fairly early in the preparatory program. The accessibility of such schools, as well as the fact that they were under college control, greatly facilitated the working out of such advantageous arrangements. Some institutions, without campus schools

[10] For further details respecting student teaching, see *The College and Teacher Education*, Chapter V *passim* and pp. 180–211; *State Programs for the Improvement of Teacher Education*, Chapter VIII, and *Evaluation in Teacher Education*, Chapter VI.

Commission on Teacher Education

of their own, were able to provide substitute facilities through agreements effected to mutual satisfaction with public schools located in their immediate neighborhoods. In either case instructors in various courses found it desirable to complement and strengthen their classroom programs by bringing their students, both in groups and individually, into direct contact with boys and girls in a variety of real school situations.

Another type of arrangement, calling for close contacts with children at a fairly early stage, should also be mentioned. According to this, sophomores or juniors gave an afternoon or evening a week during a quarter or semester to assisting in the work of local youth-serving agencies. These experiences with boys and girls in nonschool situations proved to have many values. They were often helpful in connection with selection, demonstrating to certain underclassmen that work with young people was unlikely to yield them personal satisfactions, while strengthening the vocational purposes of others. They also tied in effectively with courses in child growth and development. The fact that the contacts provided were away from school had its own advantages: children are never merely *school* children, and teachers who have come to understand what they are like when they are elsewhere are better equipped than those who lack such knowledge.

An ingenious arrangement, already mentioned, was that whereby a considerable proportion of the prospective teachers at one university was enabled to spend several weeks just prior to the opening of the sophomore year helping out full time in various public schools. In this way an unusually early concentrated experience with school and community realities was provided. Students were prepared for the event during their freshman year, plans were worked out carefully in advance by faculty members and school administrators working together, and the students' experiences were definitely drawn on in connection with courses immediately following. Of course, the work assigned in the field was very different from that given when, toward the end of their preparatory course, the undergraduates undertook responsible student teaching; but it proved possible to find many things for them to do that were educationally valuable to them as individuals as well as useful to the host schools.

Increased use of direct experience prior to student teaching proper had, as has been seen, the valuable effect of leading more course instructors to familiarize themselves with real school situations. This strengthened the likelihood that their instruction would provide a realistic foundation for student teaching. A related development was the tendency for these instructors to play an increased role in the planning and oversight of such teaching, to provide counseling services for undergraduates while in the field, and to share in the conduct of seminars after teaching experience, focused on problems met by students while in the schools. Many values of early direct experience to the students have already been mentioned. Here one more may be specified: prospective teachers with such experience came to responsible student teaching with much more self-confidence and ease than those whose prior contacts with flesh-and-blood youngsters had been slight.

STUDENT TEACHING PROPER

The arrangements made for actual student teaching varied widely in the cooperative study, notably reflecting differences in local circumstance. There was a distinct tendency, however, to lead up to culminating full-time experience, throughout periods ranging from three to nine weeks, in more or less typical off-campus schools. The colleges and universities that possessed campus schools or adequate substitutes therefor customarily used them for beginning student teaching, but even these were tending to send their students into the field for at least part of their professional practice. The full-time arrangement made it possible for prospective teachers to get the feel of whole-school situations and often of community situations as well. Moreover, it made it easier to ensure student teaching experiences in rural and other situations similar to those in which the prospective teachers were likely to find employment after graduation.

Relatively concentrated and extended student teaching in typical school situations proved to have a variety of related values. It enabled prospective teachers to get really acquainted with at least a few children, to observe them fairly closely in different situations—often including their homes—and to discover for themselves the significance of teacher-pupil relationships. It also made possible getting the feel of a school as a whole, of the relations existing among teachers and between them and administrative officers and parents, all this yielding some sense of the significance for educational accomplishment of the degree of institutional unity existing. Finally, it provided opportunity for community study, for finding out at first hand something about the school-community interplay and its significance for the teacher's work. Experience in rural communities, frequently especially arranged for, had particular advantages for the large proportion of students who could look forward to beginning their active careers in such settings.

Often during such practice-teaching periods students returned to the campus on Saturdays for seminar discussions with their instructors. Thus was provided prompt opportunity to consider the implications of new experiences and to receive guidance as to how to handle troublesome situations. Of course, students likewise had continuous supervision from particular directing teachers in the schools and were ordinarily also visited on the job by representatives of the college. Finally, it was normal practice to set up a special seminar during the semester or quarter following full-time field experience, in which questions growing out of the students' contacts could be carefully considered. Faculty members representing the various academic fields as well as the more professional subjects took part in these seminars. One frequent result was that the ideas of members of both groups as to how their earlier courses should be conducted were significantly affected.

TIME ALLOCATIONS IN TEACHER EDUCATION

One of the problems that continually recurs with respect to programs of teacher preparation is that of the allocation of available time to the various elements. It is usual for every faculty member to feel that more attention might advantageously be devoted to his particular specialty. This view tends to grow stronger with the steady cumulation of knowledge and the consequent tendency for each subject to be broken down into more and more subspecialties, the proper teaching of each of which seems to call for more and more time. It undoubtedly gains further support from the tendency of each specialist to identify with his subject. Nor is the competitive influence of departmentalism to be overlooked.

The Commission has already expressed the opinion that joint study by faculty members of the needs of students and communities, and of the problems of the schools, in each case broadly viewed, is likely to help bring agreement as to the pattern of teacher preparation. It has also taken the position that at least three-eighths of the total time of a four-year program should be given to work designed primarily to promote the ends of general education. It believes that from one-eighth to one-sixth of that total time will ordinarily suffice for strictly professional instruction. But it is impressed by the fact that many courses, especially those of newer type, are not easily assigned to some particular category: for example, a course on the community has implications for both general and professional education and in the case of prospective teachers of the social studies for subject-matter equipment as well. The Commission does not believe that nationwide agreement as to the allocation of time in programs of teacher education is desirably to be sought; for it prefers to emphasize the values of more genuinely participant and realistic local study of the problem, as well as of cooperative study in which state departments of education and representatives of the state's institutions of higher learning democratically share.[11]

[11] See *The Improvement of Teacher Education,* Chapter IV, pp. 192–218.

MERLE L. BORROWMAN, Professor of Education and History at the University of Wisconsin, was born in Idaho Falls, Idaho, in 1920. He received his B.A. from Brigham Young University, his M.A. from the University of Idaho, and his Ed.D. from Teachers College, Columbia University. Professor Borrowman has taught at Teachers College and the University of Hawaii, and was consultant to James Bryant Conant during the writing of *The Education of American Teachers*. His previous publications include *The Liberal and Technical in Teacher Education* (1956).